2018 SQA Specimen and Past Papers with Answers

Higher
GEOGRAPHY

2016 & 2018 Exams
and 2018 Specimen Question Paper

HODDER
GIBSON
AN HACHETTE UK COMPANY

This book contains the official SQA 2016 and 2018, and the 2018 Specimen Question Paper for Higher Geography, with associated SQA-approved answers modified from the official marking instructions that accompany the paper.

In addition the book contains study skills advice. This advice has been specially commissioned by Hodder Gibson, and has been written by experienced senior teachers and examiners in line with the new Higher syllabus and assessment outlines. This is not SQA material but has been devised to provide further guidance for Higher examinations.

Hodder Gibson is grateful to the copyright holders, as credited on the final page of the Answer section, for permission to use their material. Every effort has been made to trace the copyright holders and to obtain their permission for the use of copyright material. Hodder Gibson will be happy to receive information allowing us to rectify any error or omission in future editions.

Hachette UK's policy is to use papers that are natural, renewable and recyclable products and made from wood grown in sustainable forests. The logging and manufacturing processes are expected to conform to the environmental regulations of the country of origin.

Orders: please contact Bookpoint Ltd, 130 Park Drive, Milton Park, Abingdon, Oxon OX14 4SE. Telephone: (44) 01235 827827. Fax: (44) 01235 400454. Lines are open 9.00–5.00, Monday to Saturday, with a 24-hour message answering service. Visit our website at www.hoddereducation.co.uk. Hodder Gibson can also be contacted directly at hoddergibson@hodder.co.uk

This collection first published in 2018 by
Hodder Gibson, an imprint of Hodder Education,
An Hachette UK Company
211 St Vincent Street
Glasgow G2 5QY

Typeset by Aptara, Inc.

Printed in the UK

A catalogue record for this title is available from the British Library

ISBN: 978-1-5104-5703-4

2 1

2019 2018

Introduction

Higher Geography

This book of SQA past papers contains the question papers used in the 2016 and 2018 exams (with the answers at the back of the book). A specimen question paper reflecting the content and duration of the revised exam from 2019 is also included. Questions from the 2017 past paper have been used to create this new specimen question paper. To avoid duplication and provide you with optimum variety of questions, we have intentionally included the 2016 past paper instead. All of the question papers included in the book provide excellent representative practice for the final exams.

Using these papers as part of your revision will help you to develop the vital skills and techniques needed for the exam, and will help you to identify any knowledge gaps you may have.

It is always a very good idea to refer to SQA's website for the most up-to-date course specification documents. These are available at www.sqa.org.uk/sqa/45627

The Course

To gain the course award, you must pass the learning outcomes for all three units as well as the course assessment. The purpose of the course assessment is to assess added value of the course, confirm attainment and provide a grade.

Course assessment

The course assessment has three components:

1. Exam question paper 1: Physical and human environments – worth 100 marks (scaled mark 50), which will last 1 hour and 50 minutes.
2. Exam question paper 2: Global issues and geographical skills – worth 60 marks (scaled mark 30), which will last 1 hour and 10 minutes.
3. The assignment – worth 30 marks, which will last 1 hour and 30 minutes.

Component 1 – Question paper 1: Physical and human environments

The question papers are set and marked by SQA, and conducted in centres under exam conditions. This question paper has 100 marks out of a total 190 marks. This is scaled by SQA to represent 46% of the overall marks for the course assessment.

This question paper enables you to demonstrate the application of your skills, knowledge and understanding from the physical and human environments sections of the course.

This question paper has two sections:

- **Section 1: Physical Environments – 50 marks consisting of extended-response questions.**
  Candidates must answer all questions in this section.

- **Section 2: Human Environments – 50 marks consisting of extended-response questions.**
  Candidates must answer all questions in this section.

Component 2 – Question paper 2: Global issues and geographical skills

This question paper has 60 marks out of a total 190 marks. This is scaled by SQA to represent 27% of the overall marks for the course assessment.

This question paper enables you to demonstrate the application of your skills, knowledge and understanding from across the global issues and geographical skills sections of the course.

This question paper has two sections:

- **Section 1: Global issues – 40 marks consisting of ___ questions.**

Candidates can choose two from the four questions. Each question is worth 20 marks.

- **Section 2: Application of geographical skills – 20 marks consisting of a mandatory extended-response question.**
  Candidates apply geographical skills acquired during course. The skills assessed in the question include mapping skills and the use of numerical/graphical information.

Component 3 – The Assignment

The purpose of the assignment is to show challenge and application by demonstrating skills, knowledge and understanding within the context of a geographical topic or issue. Candidates can choose the topic or issue to be researched.

This assignment provides candidates with the opportunity to demonstrate higher-order cognitive skills and knowledge of methods and techniques.

- The assignment involves identifying a geographical topic or issue.
- It also involves carrying out research, which should include fieldwork where appropriate.
- Candidates will be asked to demonstrate knowledge of the suitability of the methods and/or reliability of the sources used.
- The assignment will involve drawing on detailed knowledge and understanding of the topic or issue.
- It will also involve analysing and processing information from a range of sources.
- It will require reaching a conclusion supported by a range of evidence on a geographical topic or issue.
- Candidates should demonstrate the skill of communicating information.

The assignment is set by centres within SQA guidelines, and the assessment is conducted under a high level of supervision and control by the presenting centre. The production of evidence for assessment will be conducted within 1 hour and 30 minutes and with the use of specified resources. This evidence is then submitted to SQA for external marking.

The assignment component of the course assessment will have **a greater emphasis on the assessment of skills** than the question paper.

Layout of this Book

This book contains two exam papers and one specimen question paper. The layout, paper colour and question level are all similar to the actual exam that you will sit, so that you are familiar with what the exam paper will look like.

The answer section is at the back of the book. Each answer contains a worked-out answer or solution so that you can see how to arrive at the right answer. The answers also include practical tips on how to tackle certain types of questions, details of how marks are awarded and advice on just what the examiners will be looking for.

As well as your class notes and textbooks, these exam papers are a useful revision tool because they will help you to get used to answering exam-style questions. You may find as you work through the questions that they refer to a case study or an example that you haven't come across before. Don't worry! You should be able to transfer your knowledge of a topic or theme to a new example. The enhanced answer section at the back will demonstrate how to read and interpret the question to identify the topic being examined and how to apply your course knowledge in order to answer the question successfully.

Examination Hints

- Make sure that you have read the instructions in the question carefully and that you have avoided needless errors such as answering the wrong sections, failing to explain when asked to or perhaps omitting to refer to a named area or case study.
- If you are asked for a named country or city, make sure you include details of any case study you have covered.
- Avoid vague answers when asked for detail. For example, avoid vague terms such as "dry soils" or "fertile soils". Instead, try to provide more detailed information in your answer such as "deep and well-drained soils" or "rich in nutrients".
- If you are given data in the form of maps, diagrams and tables in the question, make sure you refer to this information in your answer to support any points of view that you give.
- Be guided by the number of marks for a question as to the length of your answer.
- Make sure that you leave yourself sufficient time to answer all of the questions.
- One technique which you might find helpful, especially when answering long questions, is to "brainstorm" possible points for your answer. You can write these down in a list at the start of your answer and cross them out as you go through them.
- If you have any time left in the exam, use it to go back over your answers to see if you can add anything to what you have written by way of additional text or including more examples or diagrams which you may have omitted.

Common Errors

Lack of sufficient detail

- This often occurs in Higher case study answers, especially in questions with high marks.
- Many candidates fail to provide sufficient detail in answers, often by omitting reference to specific examples, or by failing to elaborate or develop points made in their answer.
- Remember that you have to give more information in your answers to gain a mark.

Irrelevant answers

- You must read the question instructions carefully to avoid giving answers which are irrelevant.
- For example, if asked to explain and you simply describe you will not score marks. If asked for a named example and you do not provide one, you will forfeit marks.

Statement reversals

- Occasionally, questions involve opposites. For example, some answers would say "death rates are high in developing countries due to poor health care" and then go on to say "death rates are low in developed countries due to good health care". Avoid doing this. You are simply stating the reverse of the first statement.
- A better second statement might be that "high standards of hygiene, health and education in developed countries have helped to bring about low death rates".

Repetition

- You should be careful not to repeat points already made in your answer. These will not gain any further marks. You may feel that you have written a long answer, but it could contain the same basic information repeated

over and over. Unfortunately, these statements will be recognised and ignored when your paper is marked.

Listing

- If you give a simple list of points rather than fuller statements in your answer, you may lose marks, for example, in a 5-mark question you will obtain only 1 mark for a list.

Bullet points

- The same rule applies to a simple list of bullet points. However, if you give bullet points with some detailed explanation, you could achieve full marks.

Types of Questions and Command Words

In these past papers, and in the exam itself, a number of command words will be used in the different types of questions you will encounter. The command words are used to show you how you should answer a question; some words indicate that you should write more than others. If you familiarise yourself with these command words, it will help you to structure your answers more effectively. The question types to look out for are listed below.

Explain

These questions ask you to explain and give reasons, for example, "strategies" and relationships. If resources are provided in the question, make sure you refer to them in your answer. Some marks may be allowed for description but these will be quite restricted.

Analyse

This involves identifying parts and the relationships between them by showing the links between different components and related concepts, noting similarities and differences, explaining possible consequences and implications, and explaining the impact of, for example, processes of degradation, strategies adopted to control events and government policies on people and the environment.

Evaluate

This will involve making judgements on, for example, the relative success or failure of strategies and projects such as a river basin management scheme or aid programmes.

Discuss

These questions ask you to develop your thoughts, for example, on a specific project or change in specified situations. You may be asked to consider both sides of an argument and provide a range of comments on each viewpoint.

Geographical Skills

This question is designed to examine your geographical skills. You will be given an Ordnance Survey map along with a variety of other resources which might include a climate graph, information table, newspaper article, statistics and photographs. You will be given a set of conditions to follow; these should be used to help you answer the question. You should use/evaluate the information you have been given to make judgements and back up your answer with map evidence, information from the diagrams and tables, etc. Remember the diagrams and OS map are there for a purpose and contain valuable information that you should incorporate in your answer!

Good luck!

Remember that the rewards for passing Higher Geography are well worth it! Your pass will help you get the future you want for yourself. In the exam, be confident in your own ability. Watch your time and pace yourself carefully. If yo[...] how to answer a question, trust your in[...] go anyway — keep calm and [...]

Study Skills – what you need to know to pass exams!

General exam revision: 20 top tips

When preparing for exams, it is easy to feel unsure of where to start or how to revise. This guide to general exam revision provides a good starting place, and, as these are very general tips, they can be applied to all your exams.

1. Start revising in good time.

Don't leave revision until the last minute – this will make you panic and it will be difficult to learn. Make a revision timetable that counts down the weeks to go.

2. Work to a study plan.

Set up sessions of work spread through the weeks ahead. Make sure each session has a focus and a clear purpose. What will you study, when and why? Be realistic about what you can achieve in each session, and don't be afraid to adjust your plans as needed.

3. Make sure you know exactly when your exams are.

Get your exam dates from the SQA website and use the timetable builder tool to create your own exam schedule. You will also get a personalised timetable from your school, but this might not be until close to the exam period.

4. Make sure that you know the topics that make up each course.

Studying is easier if material is in manageable chunks – why not use the SQA topic headings or create your own from your class notes? Ask your teacher for help on this if you are not sure.

5. Break the chunks up into even smaller bits.

The small chunks should be easier to cope with. Remember that they fit together to make larger ideas. Even the process of chunking down will help!

6. Ask yourself these key questions for each course:

- Are all topics compulsory or are there choices?
- Which topics seem to come up time and time again?
- Which topics are your strongest and which are your weakest?

Use your answers to these questions to work out how much time you will need to spend revising each topic.

7. Make sure you know what to expect in the exam.

The subject-specific introduction to this book will help with this. Make sure you can answer these questions:

- How is the paper structured?
- How much time is there for each part of the exam?
- What types of question are involved? These will vary depending on the subject so read the subject-specific section carefully.

8. Past papers are a vital revision tool!

Use past papers to support your revision wherever possible. This book contains the answers and mark schemes too – refer to these carefully when checking your work. Using the mark scheme is useful; even if you don't manage to get all the marks available first time when you first practise, it helps you identify how to extend and develop your answers to get more marks next time – and of course, in the real exam.

9. Use study methods that work well for you.

People study and learn in different ways. Reading and looking at diagrams suits some students. Others prefer to listen and hear material – what about reading out loud or getting a friend or family member to do this for you? You could also record and play back material.

10. There are three tried and tested ways to make material stick in your long-term memory:

- Practising – e.g. rehearsal, repeating
- Organising – e.g. making drawings, lists, diagrams, tables, memory aids
- Elaborating – e.g. incorporating the material into a story or an imagined journey

11. Learn actively.

Most people prefer to learn actively – for example, making notes, highlighting, redrawing and redrafting, making up memory aids, or writing past paper answers. A good way to stay engaged and inspired is to mix and match these methods – find the combination that best suits you. This is likely to vary depending on the topic or subject.

12. Be an expert.

Be sure to have a few areas in which you feel you are an expert. This often works because at least some of them will come up, which can boost confidence.

13. Try some visual methods.

Use symbols, diagrams, charts, flashcards, post-it notes etc. Don't forget – the brain takes in chunked images more easily than loads of text.

14. Remember – practice makes perfect.

Work on difficult areas again and again. Look and read – then test yourself. You cannot do this too much.

15. Try past papers against the clock.

Practise writing answers in a set time. This is a good habit from the start but is especially important when you get closer to exam time.

16. Collaborate with friends.

Test each other and talk about the material – this can really help. Two brains are better than one! It is amazing how talking about a problem can help you solve it.

17. Know your weaknesses.

Ask your teacher for help to identify what you don't know. Try to do this as early as possible. If you are having trouble, it is probably with a difficult topic, so your teacher will already be aware of this – most students will find it tough.

18. Have your materials organised and ready.

Know what is needed for each exam:

- Do you need a calculator or a ruler?
- Should you have pencils as well as pens?
- Will you need water or paper tissues?

19. Make full use of school resources.

Find out what support is on offer:

- Are there study classes available?
- When is the library open?
- When is the best time to ask for extra help?
- Can you borrow textbooks, study guides, past papers, etc.?
- Is school open for Easter revision?

20. Keep fit and healthy!

Try to stick to a routine as much as possible, including with sleep. If you are tired, sluggish or dehydrated, it is difficult to see how concentration is even possible. Combine study with relaxation, drink plenty of water, eat sensibly, and get fresh air and exercise – all these things will help more than you could imagine. Good luck!

HIGHER

2016

National Qualifications 2016

X733/76/11

Geography

FRIDAY, 6 MAY

9:00 AM – 11:15 AM

Total marks — 60

SECTION 1 — PHYSICAL ENVIRONMENTS — 15 marks

Attempt ALL questions.

SECTION 2 — HUMAN ENVIRONMENTS — 15 marks

Attempt ALL questions.

SECTION 3 — GLOBAL ISSUES — 20 marks

Attempt TWO questions.

SECTION 4 — APPLICATION OF GEOGRAPHICAL SKILLS — 10 marks

Attempt the question.

Credit will be given for appropriately labelled sketch maps and diagrams.

Write your answers clearly in the answer booklet provided. In the answer booklet you must clearly identify the question number you are attempting.

Use **blue** or **black** ink.

Before leaving the examination room you must give your answer booklet to the Invigilator; if you do not you may lose all the marks for this paper.

MARKS

SECTION 1 — PHYSICAL ENVIRONMENTS — 15 marks
Attempt ALL questions

Question 1

Study Maps Q1A and Q1B before answering this question.

(a) **Compare** the rainfall patterns across West Africa; **and**

(b) **suggest reasons** for the variations.　　　　　　　　　　　　　　　　　5

Map Q1A: Location of selected air masses and the ITCZ in January and July

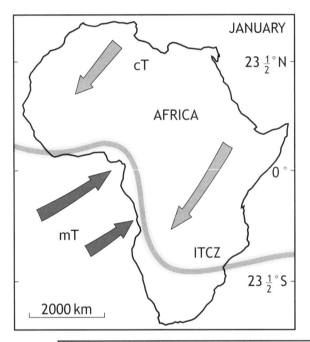
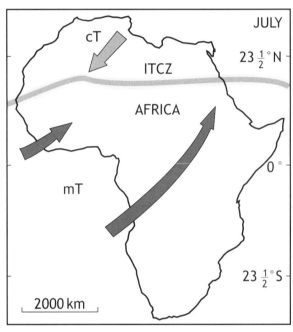

Key:		
mT = Maritime Tropical		cT = Continental Tropical
ITCZ = Inter Tropical Convergence Zone		

MARKS

Question 1 (continued)

Map Q1B: Rainfall patterns in West Africa

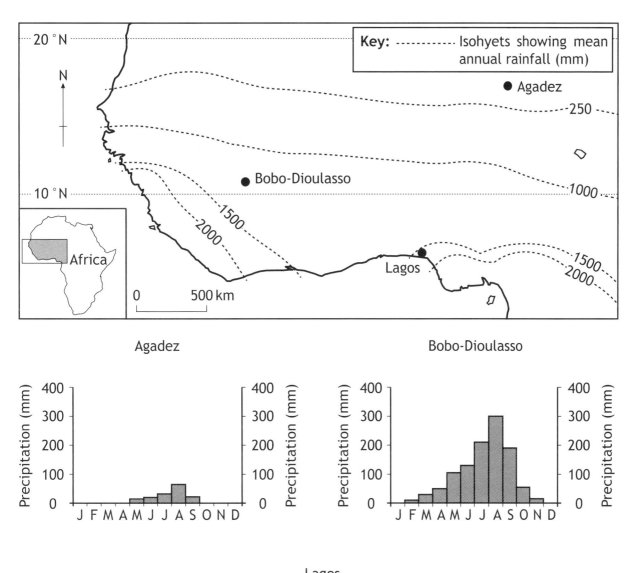

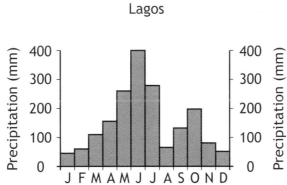

[Turn over

MARKS

Question 2

Read Diagram Q2.

Diagram Q2: Extract from Lake District Management Plan

The Lake District's varied scenery and historic environment provide for a wide range of sport, recreational and leisure activities . . . this has grown and changed over time.

As the National Park continues to change, we need to monitor how access and recreation is being managed to ensure that a balance exists between the needs of everyone.

State of the Park Report 2005: Access and Recreation

Referring to a glaciated upland area you have studied:

(a)   **explain** the environmental conflicts caused by the various land uses   ;   **5**

(b)   (i)   **explain** the strategies used to manage these conflicts; and

        (ii) **comment on** the effectiveness of these strategies.   **5**

MARKS

SECTION 2 — HUMAN ENVIRONMENTS — 15 marks

Attempt ALL questions

Question 3

Look at Map Q3 before answering this question.

The Great Green Wall Initiative aims to reduce the impact of land degradation in the Sahel zone of Northern Africa.

(a)　**Explain** techniques employed to manage rural land degradation in a rainforest **or** semi arid area that you have studied; **and**

(b)　**comment on** the effectiveness of these techniques.　　　　　　　　　　　　6

Map Q3: The Great Green Wall Initiative

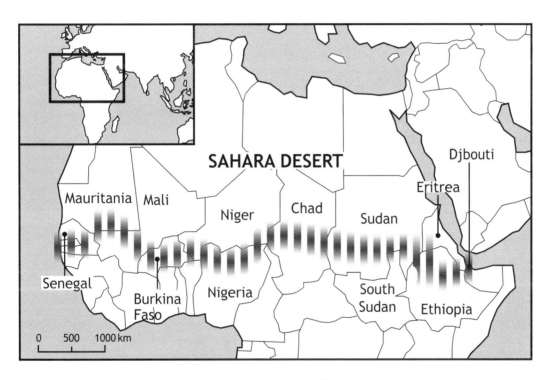

　　　　█ █ █　"Great Green Wall" of trees

　　　　　　　Total distance: 7,775 km

　　　　　　　Total area: 11,662,500 hectares

[Turn over

MARKS

Question 4

In November 2013, the Chairperson of Nigeria's National Population Commission resigned after questioning the accuracy of the data gathered about the country's population.

(a) **Discuss** how countries gather accurate population data. 3

(b) **Explain** why it is difficult to gather accurate population data in developing world countries. 6

SECTION 3 — GLOBAL ISSUES — 20 marks
Attempt TWO questions

[Turn over

Question 5: River Basin Management

Map Q5A: Bangladesh

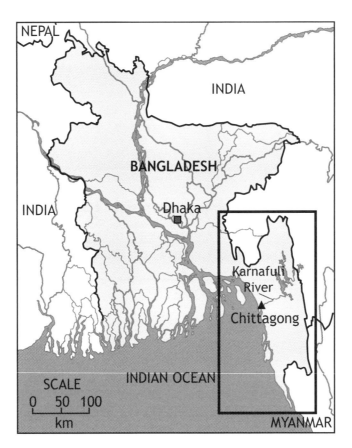

Map Q5B: Karnafuli River Basin

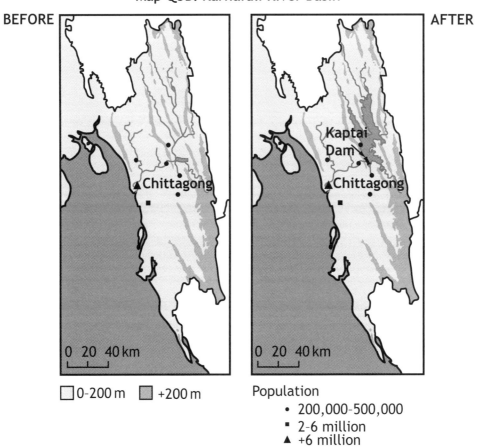

MARKS

Question 5: (continued)

Diagram Q5A: Climate Graph, Chittagong, Bangladesh

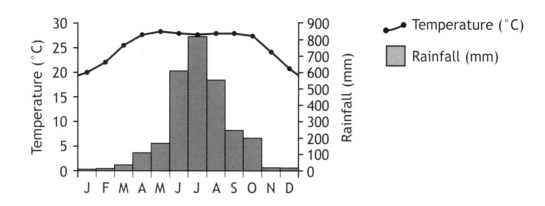

Diagram Q5B: Population growth in Bangladesh

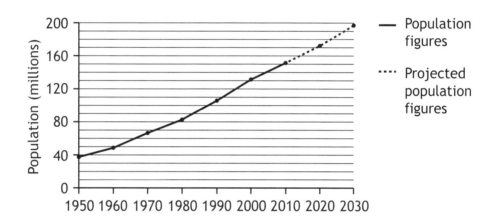

Diagram Q5C: Selected statistics, Bangladesh

Access to Improved drinking water	84%
Access to Improved sanitation	55%
Access to Electricity	62%
Main Industries	Textiles; Agriculture (rice/jute); Construction

(a)　Study Map Q5A, Map Q5B, Diagram Q5A, Diagram Q5B, and Diagram Q5C.

　　　Explain why there is a need for water management in the Karnafuli River Basin.　　6

(b)　Referring to a water control project you have studied, **discuss** the positive **and** negative **environmental** impacts created by the construction of a major dam and its associated reservoir.　　4

[Turn over

Question 6: Development and Health

Look at Table Q6.

Table Q6: Selected Developing Countries

Country	GNI (Gross National Income) per capita (US$)
Venezuela	13,600
Nigeria	2,800
Malawi	900

(a) **Explain** why using only **one** development indicator, such as Gross National Income (GNI) per capita, may fail to reflect accurately the true quality of life within a country.   3

(b) Referring to specific Primary Health Care strategies you have studied:

   (i) **explain** how these strategies meet the health care needs of the people in a developing country; **and**

   (ii) **comment on** the effectiveness of these strategies.   7

MARKS

Question 7: Global Climate Change

(a)   **Explain** the **physical** causes of climate change.   4

(b)   Study Diagram Q7.

      Explain possible strategies for managing climate change.   6

Diagram Q7: Levels of managing Climate Change

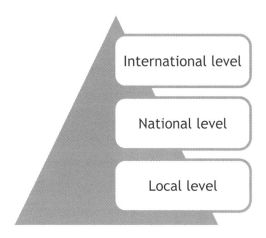

[Turn over

MARKS

Question 8: Trade, Aid and Geopolitics

Table Q8: Trade Patterns of Selected Countries

Country	Population (millions)	GDP per Capita (US$)	Exports (billions US$)	Imports (billions US$)	Balance of Trade (billions US$)
Australia	23	67,304	252	245	+7
USA	318	51,704	1,575	2,273	−698
Germany	81	41,866	1,493	1,233	+260
UK	64	39,161	475	646	−171
Saudi Arabia	30	24,524	376	147	+229
Botswana	2	16,400	3	7	−4
Russia	144	14,302	515	341	+174
Brazil	201	11,358	245	241	+4
South Africa	53	7,525	91	99	−8
China	1,361	6,071	2,210	1,772	+438
Ghana	25	3,500	13	18	−5
India	1,241	1,499	318	516	−198
Zimbabwe	13	600	7	4	+3

(Data from CIA World Fact book − 2013)

(a)   Study Table Q8 above.

   To what extent does the data in the table show inequalities in the pattern of world trade?   4

(b)   **Give reasons** for the inequalities in the pattern of trade shown in the table or between other countries that you have studied.   6

Question 9: Energy   MARKS

Graph Q9A: Total UK energy consumption (1970-2030)

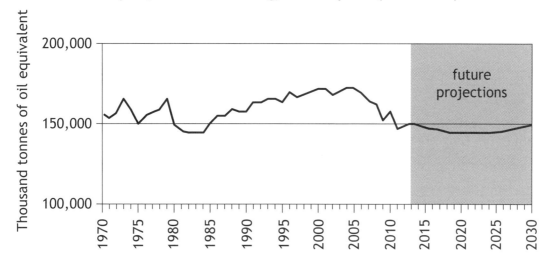

(a)   Look at Graph Q9A above.

Suggest reasons for the changes in energy consumption in the UK.   5

Diagram Q9B: Hydraulic Fracturing ("Fracking") to extract shale gas

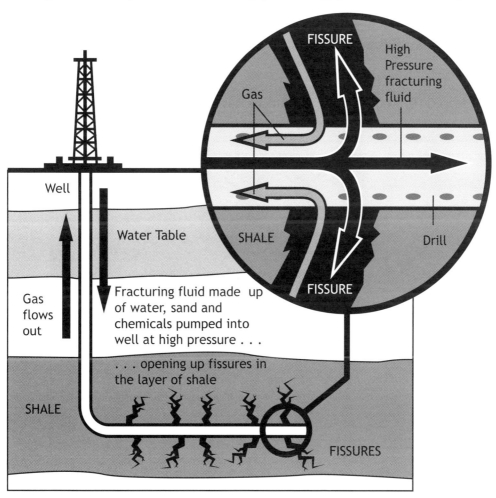

(b)   Look carefully at Diagram Q9B above.

Discuss the advantages **and** disadvantages of hydraulic fracturing ("fracking"), or
any other **non**-renewable source of energy you have studied, in meeting the energy
demands of a country.   5

[Turn over

MARKS

SECTION 4 — APPLICATION OF GEOGRAPHICAL SKILLS — 10 marks
Attempt the question

Question 10

East Sussex County Council is building a new by-pass from 743091 to 776111 (The Bexhill–Hastings Link Road), however, not everyone is pleased with this decision.

Study the OS Map (Extract No 2214/EXP124: Hastings and Bexhill), Map Q10, Diagram Q10A, Diagram Q10B, Diagram Q10C and Diagram Q10D, before answering this question.

Referring to evidence from the OS map extract, and other information from the sources, **discuss**:

(a)   the advantages **and** disadvantages of the proposed route; **and**

(b)   any possible impacts on the surrounding area.

10

Diagram Q10A: Part of Sussex Wildlife Trust's response to the new road proposal

"Sussex Wildlife Trust strongly objects to the Bexhill–Hastings Link Road Scheme. The proposals do not represent sustainable development. The scheme will result in unacceptable environmental damage."

Map Q10: Route of the Bexhill to Hastings Link Road

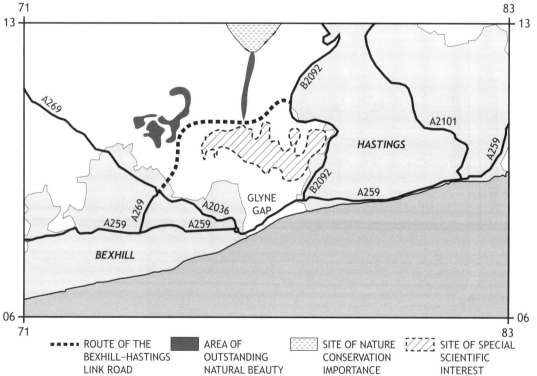

Question 10 (continued)   MARKS

Diagram Q10B: Average Hourly Traffic Flow on the A259 at Glyne Gap 768082 June 2012

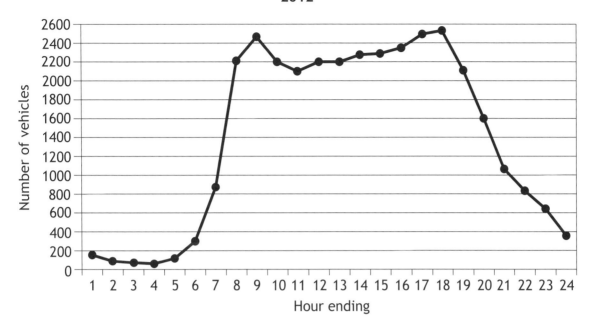

Diagram Q10C: Number of days that safe air pollution levels were exceeded at Glyne Gap 768082 June 2011 to June 2013

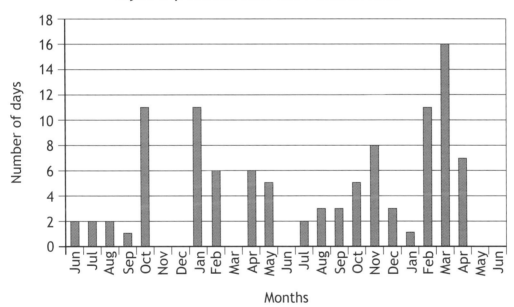

Diagram Q10D: Predicted visual impact on the Combe Havan Valley (View East from 757107) towards Adam's farm

Current View	Artist impression of view in 2020

[END OF QUESTION PAPER]

[BLANK PAGE]

DO NOT WRITE ON THIS PAGE

National
Qualifications
2016

X733/76/21

Geography
Ordnance Survey Map

FRIDAY, 6 MAY

9:00 AM – 11:15 AM

ORDNANCE SURVEY MAP

For Question 10

Note: The colours used in the printing of this map extract are indicated in the four little boxes at the top of the map extract. Each box should contain a colour; if any does not, the map is incomplete and should be returned to the Invigilator.

Ordnance Survey

1:25 000 Scale
Explorer Series

ROADS AND PATHS   Not necessarily rights of way

M 1 or A6(M)   Motorway
A 35   Service Area   Junction Number
A 35   Dual carriageway
A 30   Main road
B 3074   Secondary road
    Narrow road with passing places
    Road under construction
    Road generally more than 4 m wide
    Road generally less than 4 m wide
    Other road, drive or track, fenced and unfenced
    Gradient: steeper than 20% (1 in 5)
        14% (1 in 7) to 20% (1 in 5)
Ferry   Ferry; Ferry P – passenger only
    Path

RAILWAYS

    Multiple track
    Single track   } Standard gauge
    Narrow gauge or Light Rapid Transit System (LRTS) and station
    Road over; road under; level crossing
    Cutting; tunnel; embankment
    Station, open to passengers; siding

PUBLIC RIGHTS OF WAY Not shown on maps of Scotland

- - - - -   Footpath
- - - - -   Bridleway
+-+-+-+   Byway open to all traffic
- - - - -   Restricted byway-not for use by mechanically propelled vehicles

The representation on this map of any other road, track or path is no evidence of the existence of a right of way

OTHER PUBLIC ACCESS

• • •   Other routes with public access

The exact nature of the rights on these routes and the existence of any restrictions may be checked with the local highway authority. Alignments are based on the best information available

◆ ◆ ◆   Recreational route
◆ ◆ ◆   National Trail / Long Distance Route
- - - - -   Permissive footpath
- - - - -   Permissive bridleway   } See note below

Footpaths and bridleways along which landowners have permitted public use but which are not rights of way. The agreement may be withdrawn.

• • •   Traffic-free cycle route
1 1   National cycle network route number – traffic free; on road

BOUNDARIES

—+—+—   National
— — —   County (England)
— — —   Unitary Authority (UA), Metropolitan District (Met Dist), London Borough (LB) or District (Scotland & Wales are solely Unitary Authorities)
....   Civil Parish (CP) (England) or Community (C) (Wales)
    National Park

HISTORICAL FEATURES

✛   Site of antiquity
⚔ 1066   Site of battle (with date)
VILLA   Roman
Castle   Non-Roman
⌂   Visible earthwork

Information provided by English Heritage for England and the Royal Commissions on the Ancient and Historical Monuments for Scotland and Wales

GENERAL FEATURES

    Gravel pit   Sand pit
    Other pit or quarry   Landfill site or slag/spoil heap
    Slopes
+   Place of worship
    Current or former place of worship
    – with tower
    – with spire, minaret or dome
☐ ☐   Building; important building
▪   Glasshouse
▲   Youth hostel
▪   Bunkhouse / camping barn / other hostel
    Bus or coach station
    Lighthouse; disused lighthouse;
    Beacon

HEIGHTS AND NATURAL FEATURES

52 ·   Ground survey height
284   Air survey height

Surface heights are to the nearest metre above mean sea level. Where two heights are shown, the first height is to the base of the triangulation pillar and the second (in brackets) to the highest natural point of the hill

    Vertical face/cliff

Boulders   Loose rock   Outcrop   Scree

    Water; mud
    Sand; sand and shingle

ACCESS LAND

DANGER AREA   Firing and test ranges in the area. Danger! Observe warning notices
MANAGED ACCESS   Access permitted within managed controls, for example, local byelaws.

England and Wales

    Access land boundary and tint
    Access land in wooded area
ℹ   Access information point

Portrayal of access land on this map is intended as a guide to land which is normally available for access on foot, for example access land created under the Countryside and Rights of Way Act 2000, and land managed by the National Trust, Forestry Commission and Woodland Trust.

Access for other activities may also exist. Some restrictions will apply; some land will be excluded from open access rights.

The depiction of rights of access does not imply or express any warranty as to its accuracy or completeness. Observe local signs and follow the Countryside Code.

Scotland

    National Trust for Scotland, always open
    National Trust for Scotland, limited access – observe local signs
    Forestry Commission Land
    Woodland Trust Land

In Scotland, everyone has access rights in law over most land and inland water, provided access is exercised responsibly (Land Reform (Scotland) Act 2003). **This includes walking, cycling, horse- riding and water access, for recreational and educational purposes, and for crossing land or water.** Access rights do not apply to motorised activities, hunting, shooting or fishing, nor if your dog is not under proper control.

TOURIST AND LEISURE INFORMATION

    Building of historic interest
    Boat trips
    Boat hire
    Cadw (Welsh heritage)
    Camp site/Caravan site
    Castle / fort
    Cathedral / Abbey
    Craft Centre
    Country park
    Cycle hire
    Cycle trail
    English Heritage property
    Fishing

    Forestry Commission visitor centre
    Garden / arboretum
    Golf course or links
    Historic Scotland
    Information centre, seasonal
    Horse riding
    Museum
    Mountain bike trail
    Nature reserve
    National Trust property
    Other tourist feature
    Parking / Park and ride, all year / seasonal
    Picnic site

    Preserved railway
PC   Public Convenience
    Public house/s
    Recreation / leisure / sports centre
    Slipway
    Telephone (public/ roadside assistance/ emergency)
    Theme / pleasure park
    Viewpoint
    Visitor centre
    Walks / trails
    Water activites
    World Heritage site or area

VEGETATION

Vegetation limits are defined by positioning of symbols

    Coniferous trees
    Non-coniferous trees
    Coppice
    Orchard
    Scrub
    Bracken, heath or rough grassland
    Marsh, reeds or saltings

    Triangulation pillar
    Mast
    Windmill; with or without sails
    Wind pump; wind turbine
pylon / pole   Electricity transmission line
BP   Boundary post
BS   Boundary stone
CG   Cattle grid
CH   Clubhouse
FB   Footbridge
MP; MS   Milepost; milestone
Mon   Monument
PO   Post office
Pol Sta   Police station
Sch   School
TH   Town hall
NTL   Normal tidal limit
·W; Spr   Well; spring

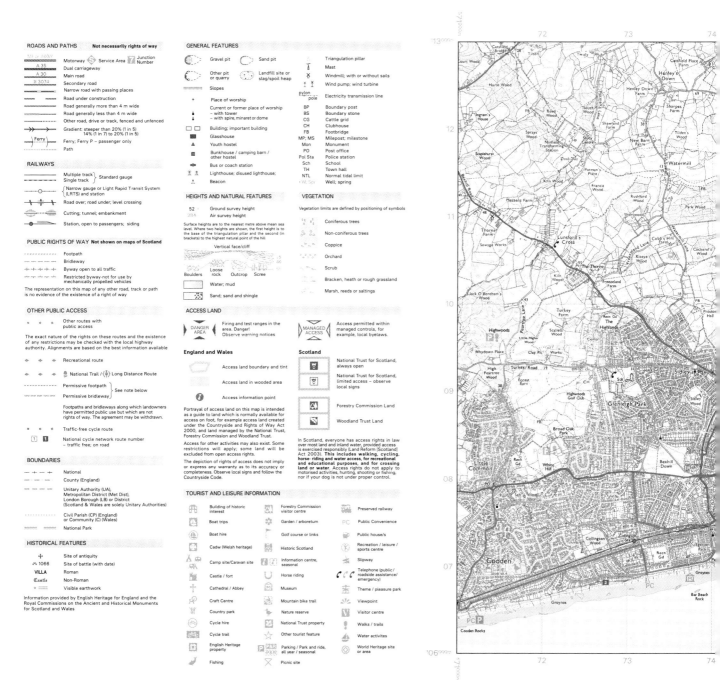

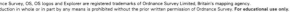

Diagrammatic only

Scale 1: 25 000

1   0 Kilometres   1

1   ¾   ½   ¼   0 Miles   1

1 kilometre = 0·6214 mile   4 centimetres to 1 kilometre (one grid square)   1 Mile = 1·6093 kilometres

[BLANK PAGE]

DO NOT WRITE ON THIS PAGE

HIGHER

2018

National Qualifications 2018

X733/76/11

Geography

TUESDAY, 1 MAY

9:00 AM — 11:15 AM

Total marks — 60

SECTION 1 — PHYSICAL ENVIRONMENTS — 15 marks

Attempt ALL questions.

SECTION 2 — HUMAN ENVIRONMENTS — 15 marks

Attempt ALL questions.

SECTION 3 — GLOBAL ISSUES — 20 marks

Attempt TWO questions.

SECTION 4 — APPLICATION OF GEOGRAPHICAL SKILLS — 10 marks

Attempt the question.

Credit will be given for appropriately labelled sketch maps and diagrams.

Write your answers clearly in the answer booklet provided. In the answer booklet you must clearly identify the question number you are attempting.

Use **blue** or **black** ink.

Before leaving the examination room you must give your answer booklet to the Invigilator; if you do not, you may lose all the marks for this paper.

MARKS

SECTION 1 — PHYSICAL ENVIRONMENTS — 15 marks
Attempt ALL questions

Question 1

'A drainage basin is an open system with four elements — **inputs**, **storage**, **transfers** *and* **outputs**.*'*

Discuss the movement of water within a drainage basin.   4

Question 2

Explain the various stages and processes involved in the formation of:

      (i) one of the features of coastal erosion and,

     (ii) one of the features of coastal deposition listed below.   7

You may wish to use diagrams.

Features of coastal erosion	Features of coastal deposition
Headland and bay	Sand bar
Wave-cut platform	Tombolo

Question 3

Diagram Q3: A typical brown earth soil profile

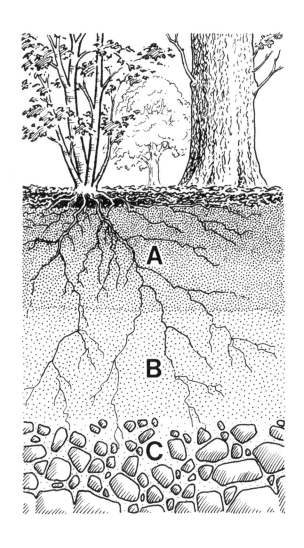

Study Diagram Q3.

Explain the main conditions and processes involved in the formation of a **brown earth** soil.   4

[Turn over

MARKS

SECTION 2 — HUMAN ENVIRONMENTS — 15 marks
Attempt ALL questions

Question 4

Diagram Q4: Photograph of Kibera shanty town, Nairobi

Look at Diagram Q4.

Evaluate the effectiveness of strategies used to improve housing in Kibera or any other developing world city you have studied.

5

MARKS

Question 5

Explain why it is difficult to gather accurate population data in developing world countries.   **6**

Question 6

Explain the strategies used to manage rural land degradation in a rainforest **or** semi-arid area that you have studied.   **4**

[Turn over

SECTION 3 — GLOBAL ISSUES — 20 marks
Attempt TWO questions

MARKS

Question 7: River basin management

(a) **Explain** the human factors which need to be considered when selecting a site for a major dam and its associated reservoir.   4

(b) Referring to a named water control project you have studied, **discuss** the socio-economic **and** environmental **benefits** created by the construction of a major dam and its associated reservoir.   6

[Turn over

MARKS

Question 8: Development and health

(a) **Suggest reasons** for the wide variations in development which exist between developing countries. You may wish to refer to countries that you have studied.   5

(b) Referring to specific examples of primary health care strategies that you have studied, **evaluate** their effectiveness in meeting the needs of people in **developing** countries.   5

MARKS

Question 9: Global climate change

(a) **Discuss** a range of possible impacts of global climate change.   **5**

(b)

Attempts are being made to both reduce greenhouse gasses and deal with the effects of climate change.

Explain possible strategies for managing climate change.   **5**

[Turn over

MARKS

Question 10: Trade, aid and geopolitics

Diagram Q10: Value of world trade by region (%)

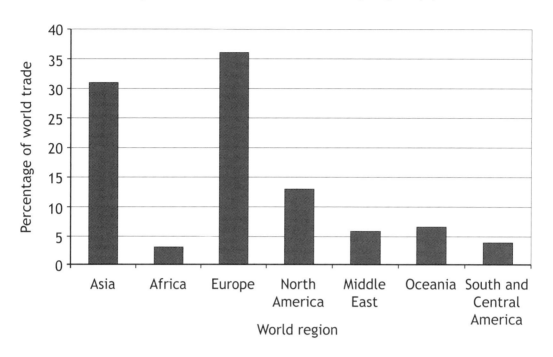

Study Diagram Q10.

(a) **Suggest** reasons for the differences in trade shown in the graph.

4

(b) **Explain** the socio-economic and environmental impacts of unfair trade on the **developing world**.

6

MARKS

Question 11: Energy

Diagram Q11: Sources of energy production for selected countries

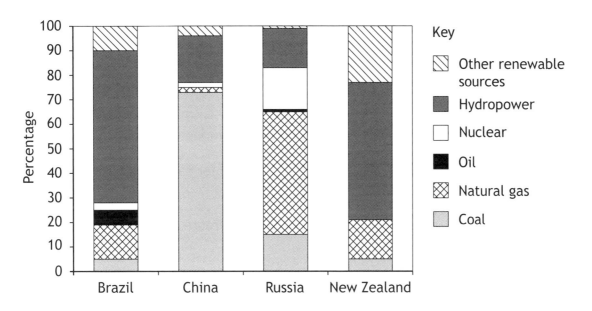

Look at Diagram Q11.

(a) **Suggest reasons** for the different methods of energy production around the world. You may wish to refer to countries you have studied.   5

(b) **Discuss** the advantages **and** disadvantages of any **non-renewable** source of energy you have studied, in meeting the energy demands of a named country.   5

[Turn over

SECTION 4 — APPLICATION OF GEOGRAPHICAL SKILLS — 10 marks

Attempt the question

MARKS

Question 12

The UK Government has given the go ahead for a second high-speed railway service, known as HS2. Phase 1 between London and Birmingham is due for completion in 2026, however not everyone is pleased with this decision.

Study the Ordnance Survey map extract of the Birmingham area; Diagram Q12a; Diagram Q12b; Diagram Q12c; and Diagram Q12d before answering this question.

Referring to evidence from the OS map extract, and other information from the sources, **discuss:**

(a) the advantages **and** disadvantages of the proposed route of the HS2 line; **and**

(b) any possible impacts on the surrounding area.

10

**Diagram Q12a: Route of high speed railway lines in England
(current and proposed)**

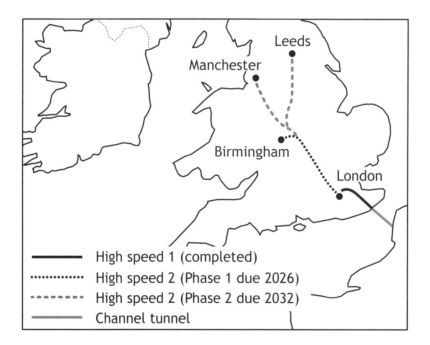

Diagram Q12b: Statement on HS2

HS2 will help accelerate the region's economic growth, for example, the global bank HSBC is building its new headquarters in Birmingham city centre, and global construction company Interserve is consolidating its operations at a new regional head office next to Birmingham International Airport. A spokesperson said:

"By 2026 Birmingham Airport will be the UK's only HS2 connected airport."

Diagram Q12c: Route map of HS2 rail line Phase 1

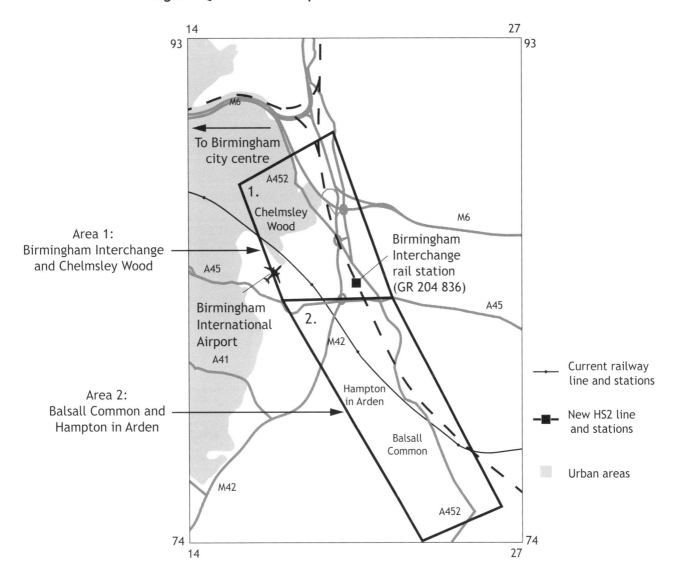

Diagram Q12d: Concerns raised by local residents in two areas

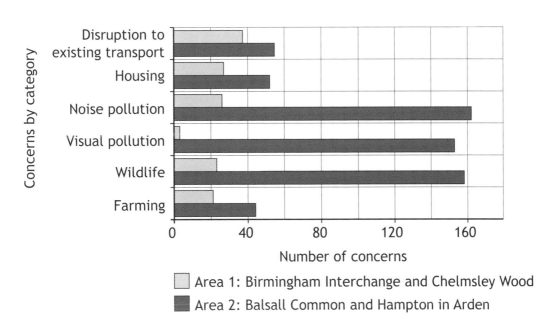

[END OF QUESTION PAPER]

Page thirteen

[BLANK PAGE]

DO NOT WRITE ON THIS PAGE

National
Qualifications
2018

X733/76/21

Geography
Ordnance Survey Map

TUESDAY, 1 MAY

9:00 AM – 11:15 AM

ORDNANCE SURVEY MAP

For Question 12

Note: The colours used in the printing of this map extract are indicated in the four little boxes at the top of the map extract. Each box should contain a colour; if any does not, the map is incomplete and should be returned to the Invigilator.

Ordnance Survey

ROADS AND PATHS

Not necessarily rights of way

Junction number

Service area — Elevated

Unfenced

A 470 — Dual carriageway

A 493 — Footbridge

B 4518

A 855 — Bridge — B 885

Motorway (dual carriageway)

Primary Route (recommended through route)

Main road

Road under construction

Secondary road

Narrow road with passing places

Road generally more than 4m wide

Road generally less than 4m wide

Path / Other road, drive or track

Gradient: steeper than 20% (1 in 5), 14% to 20% (1 in 7 to 1 in 5)

Gates, Road tunnel

Ferry P — Ferry V

Ferry (passenger), Ferry (vehicle)

RAILWAYS

Track multiple or single

Track under construction

Siding

Tunnel, cuttings

Light rapid transit system, narrow gauge or tramway

Bridges, footbridge

LC Level crossing

Viaduct, embankment

a Station, (a) principal

Light rapid transit system station

WATER FEATURES

Marsh or salting

Towpath — Lock — Slopes — Cliff

Aqueduct — Canal — Ford — Beacon — Flat rock — Shingle

Weir — Footbridge — Bridge — Normal tidal limit — Sand — Dunes — Lighthouse (disused) — Lighthouse (in use)

Canal (dry) — Mud — Low water mark — High water mark

HEIGHTS

1 metre = 3·2808 feet

Contours are at 10 metres vertical interval

·144 Heights are to the nearest metre above mean sea level

Where two heights are shown the first height is to the base of the triangulation pillar and the second (in brackets) to the highest natural point of the hill

ROCK FEATURES

Outcrop

Cliff

Scree

PUBLIC RIGHTS OF WAY

.... Footpath

– – – – Bridleway

-·-·-·-· Restricted byway

-+-+-+-+ Byway open to all traffic

The symbols show the defined route so far as the scale of mapping will allow.

The representation on this map of any other road, track or path is no evidence of the existence of a right of way. Not shown on maps of Scotland

Danger Area — Firing and Test Ranges in the area. Danger! Observe warning notices.

OTHER PUBLIC ACCESS

· · · · Other route with public access (not normally shown in urban areas). Alignments are based on the best information available. These routes are not shown on maps of Scotland.

On-road cycle route

Traffic-free cycle route

4 National Cycle Network number

8 Regional Cycle Network number

National Trail, European Long Distance Path, Long Distance Route, selected Recreational Routes

BOUNDARIES

-+- — - +- — National

-·+·-·+·- District

-·-·-·-· County, Unitary Authority, Metropolitan District or London Borough

National Park

ANTIQUITIES

+ Site of antiquity

✕ Battlefield (with date)

☆ Visible earthwork

VILLA Roman

Castle Non-Roman

TOURIST INFORMATION

Å ♙ ♙♙ Camp site / caravan site

✿ Garden

⌐ Golf course or links

i i Information centre (all year / seasonal)

⚲ Nature reserve

P P&R Parking, Park and ride (all year / seasonal)

⊼ Picnic site

✕ Recreation / leisure / sports centre

▨ Selected places of tourist interest

✆ ✆ Telephone, public / roadside assistance

☼ Viewpoint

V Visitor centre

! Walks / Trails

Ⓦ World Heritage site or area

▲ Youth hostel

LAND FEATURES

✕ — — ✕ Electricity transmission line (pylons shown at standard spacing)

> – > – > Pipe line (arrow indicates direction of flow)

Buildings

Important building (selected)

Bus or coach station

⌂ Current or former place of worship — with tower / with spire, minaret or dome

+ Place of worship

⌸ Glass structure

Ⓗ Heliport

⊼ Triangulation pillar

Ỵ Mast

Ỵ Ỵ Wind pump, wind turbine

✖ Windmill with or without sails

Graticule intersection at 5' intervals

Cutting, embankment

Landfill site or slag/spoil heap

Coniferous wood

Non-coniferous wood

Mixed wood

Orchard

Park or ornamental ground

Forestry Commission land

National Trust (always open / limited access, observe local signs)

National Trust for Scotland (always open / limited access, observe local signs)

ABBREVIATIONS

Br	Bridge	MS	Milestone
Cemy	Cemetery	Mus	Museum
CG	Cattle grid	P	Post office
CH	Clubhouse	PC	Public convenience (in rural areas)
Fm	Farm	PH	Public house
Ho	House	Sch	School
MP	Milepost	TH	Town Hall, Guildhall or equivalent

Magnetic North / True North / Grid North

Diagrammatic only

Scale 1: 50 000

2 centimetres to 1 kilometre (one grid square)

2 — 1 — 0 Kilometres — 1 — 2 — 3

1 — 0 Miles — 1 — 2

1 kilometre = 0·6214 mile

1 mile = 1·6093 kilometres

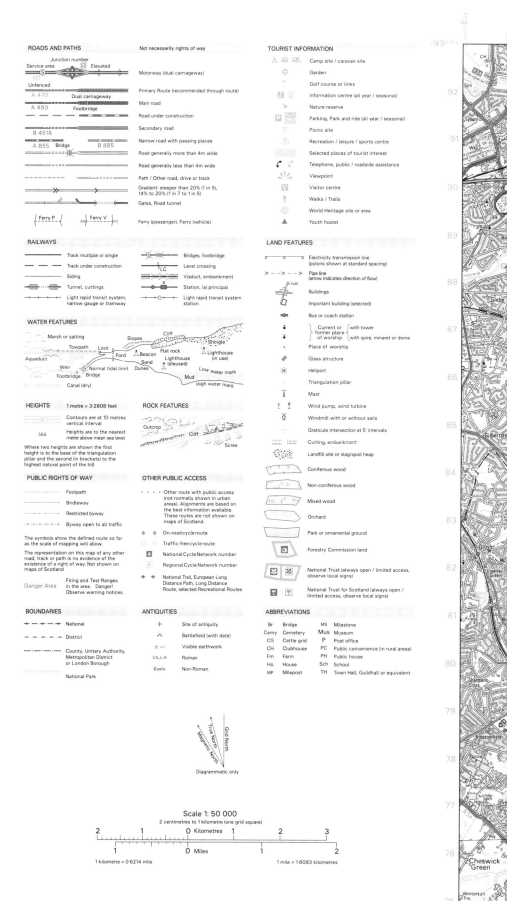

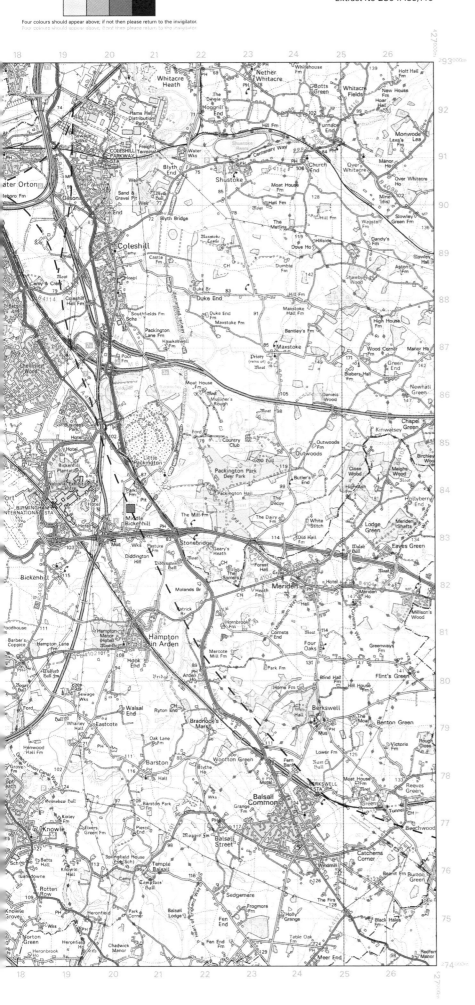

[BLANK PAGE]

DO NOT WRITE ON THIS PAGE

HIGHER

2018 Specimen
Question Paper

National
Qualifications
SPECIMEN ONLY

S833/76/11

Geography
Physical and Human
Environments

Date — Not applicable

Duration — 1 hour 50 minutes

Total marks — 100

SECTION 1 — PHYSICAL ENVIRONMENTS — 50 marks

Attempt ALL questions.

SECTION 2 — HUMAN ENVIRONMENTS — 50 marks

Attempt ALL questions.

You will receive credit for appropriately labelled sketch maps and diagrams.

Write your answers clearly in the answer booklet provided. In the answer booklet you must clearly identify the question number you are attempting.

Use **blue** or **black** ink.

Before leaving the examination room you must give your answer booklet to the Invigilator; if you do not, you may lose all the marks for this paper.

MARKS

Section 1 — PHYSICAL ENVIRONMENTS — 50 marks
Attempt ALL questions.

Question 1

Diagram Q1: A meander on the River Clyde

Look at Diagram Q1.

> Meanders are features commonly found in the middle and lower course of rivers.

Explain the formation of a meander.

You may wish to use an annotated diagram or diagrams.   8

Question 2

Diagram Q2: Flood hydrograph for the River Valency at Boscastle, 16 August 2004

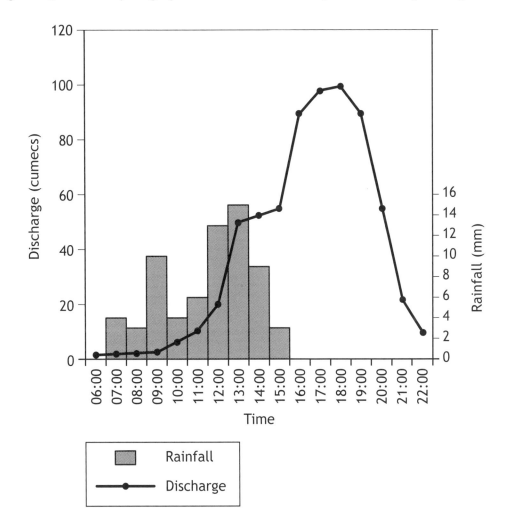

Study Diagram Q2.

For the River Valency at Boscastle on 16 August 2004:

    (a) **describe** the changes in discharge level **and**

    (b) **suggest reasons** why these changes may have occurred.　　　**10**

MARKS

Question 3

Draw a fully annotated soil profile of a **podzol** soil to show its main characteristics (including horizons, colour, texture and drainage), and associated vegetation.

8

Question 4

Diagram Q4: A ribbon lake

Look at Diagram Q4.

> Ribbon lakes are a common feature in many upland glaciated landscapes.

Explain how a ribbon lake is formed.

You may wish to use an annotated diagram or diagrams.

10

MARKS

Question 5

Diagram Q5A: The Intertropical Convergence Zone (ITCZ)

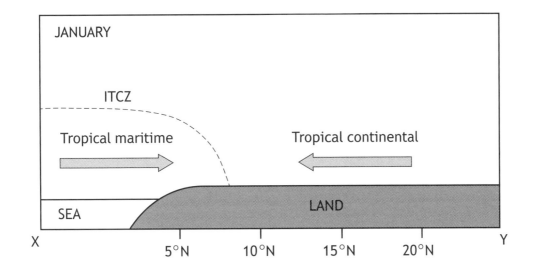

Diagram Q5B: Location of section X–Y

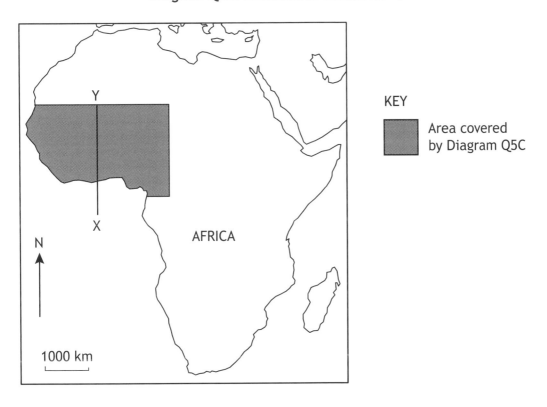

Study Diagrams Q5A and Q5B.

(a) **Describe** the origin and characteristics of the tropical maritime and tropical continental air masses.

6

Question 5 (continued)

Diagram Q5C: West Africa — mean annual rainfall

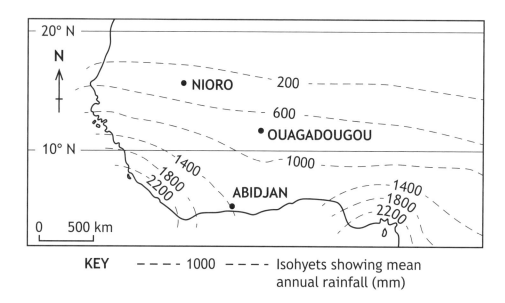

KEY – – – – 1000 – – – – Isohyets showing mean
annual rainfall (mm)

Diagram Q5D: West Africa — selected rainfall graphs

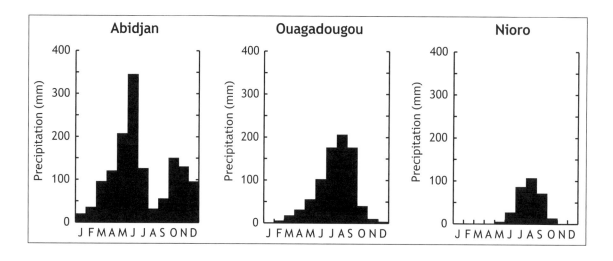

(b) Study Diagrams Q5A, Q5B, Q5C and Q5D.

Referring to the position of the ITCZ:

(i) **describe** the changing rainfall pattern as you move inland from Abidjan to Nioro **and**

(ii) **suggest reasons** for these differences.

8

MARKS

Section 2 — HUMAN ENVIRONMENTS — 50 marks

Attempt ALL questions.

Question 6

Diagram Q6: Photograph of Dharavi Slum, Mumbai, India

Look at Diagram Q6.

Rapid urbanisation in **developing** world cities has resulted in many housing problems.

Referring to a developing world city you have studied:

(a) **discuss** the socio-economic and environmental problems associated with housing in shanty towns.   6

(b) **explain** strategies used to manage these problems.   8

MARKS

Question 7

> Many glaciated and coastal areas have competing land users which can create conflict.

Referring to a glaciated upland **or** coastal area you have studied:

(a) **explain** the strategies used to manage these conflicts **and**

(b) **comment** on the effectiveness of these strategies.   10

Question 8

> In November 2013, the chairperson of Nigeria's National Population Commission resigned after questioning the accuracy of the data gathered about the country's population.

(a) **Discuss** how countries gather accurate population data.   6

(b) Referring to countries you have studied, **explain** why it is difficult to gather accurate population data in developing world countries.   12

MARKS

Question 9

Diagram Q9: Projected change in Scotland's population 2018–2038

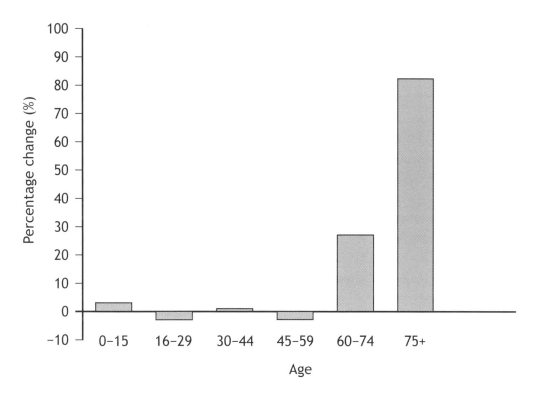

Study Diagram Q9.

(a) **Describe** the changes projected to take place in Scotland's population structure **and**

(b) **suggest** possible consequences of these changes.   8

[END OF SPECIMEN QUESTION PAPER]

[BLANK PAGE]

DO NOT WRITE ON THIS PAGE

National
Qualifications
SPECIMEN ONLY

S833/76/12

Geography
Global Issues and
Geographical Skills

Date — Not applicable

Duration — 1 hour 10 minutes

Total marks — 60

SECTION 1 — GLOBAL ISSUES — 40 marks

Attempt **TWO** questions.

SECTION 2 — APPLICATION OF GEOGRAPHICAL SKILLS — 20 marks

Attempt the question.

You will receive credit for appropriately labelled sketch maps and diagrams.

Write your answers clearly in the answer booklet provided. In the answer booklet you must clearly identify the question number you are attempting.

Use **blue** or **black** ink.

Before leaving the examination room you must give your answer booklet to the Invigilator; if you do not, you may lose all the marks for this paper.

MARKS

SECTION 1 — GLOBAL ISSUES — 40 marks

Attempt TWO questions.

Question 1: River basin management

(a) When selecting the site for a dam and its associated reservoir:

(i) **describe** the physical factors that need to be considered **and**

(ii) **explain** why they are important.   8

(b) **Discuss** the adverse socio-economic and environmental consequences of a
named river management project that you have studied.   12

Question 2: Development and health

Of the 106 countries with ongoing malaria transmission in 2000, 57 achieved reductions
in new malaria cases of at least 75% by 2015. Eighteen countries reduced their malaria
cases by 50—75%.

World Health Organization — World Malaria Report 2015.

For a water-related disease you have studied:

(a) **describe**, in detail, the strategies used to manage the disease **and**

(b) **comment** on the effectiveness of these strategies.   20

Question 3: Global climate change

The impacts of global warming are likely to be 'severe and irreversible', a major report
by the UN has warned.

Newspaper article

(a) **Discuss** a range of possible impacts of climate change. You should support your
answer with specific examples.   12

(b) Many strategies have been implemented to both reduce greenhouse gas
emissions **and** to manage the effects of climate change.

(i) **Describe** strategies you have studied **and**

(ii) **comment** on their effectiveness.   8

MARKS

Question 4: Energy

Diagram Q4A: World energy consumption 1971 and 2013

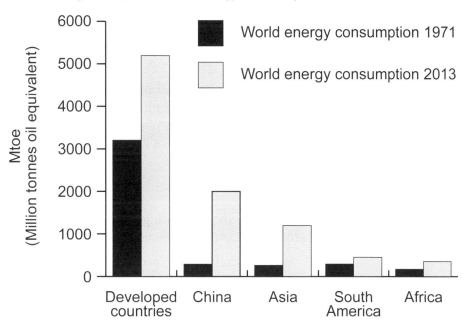

(a) Study Diagram Q4A.

   (i) **Describe** the trends shown in the graph **and**

   (ii) **suggest reasons** for these changes in energy demand.   **10**

Diagram Q4B: Norway — source of electrical generation 2012

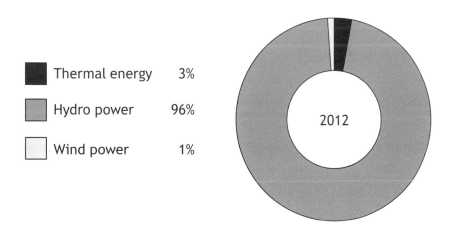

(b) Look at Diagram Q4B.

Discuss the effectiveness of hydroelectric power (HEP), or any other renewable source of energy you have studied, in meeting energy demands. You may wish to refer to one or more countries in your answer.   **10**

MARKS

SECTION 2 — APPLICATION OF GEOGRAPHICAL SKILLS — 20 marks

Attempt the question.

Question 5

> Planning permission has been granted to create 300 new homes to the south of Highbridge, which is a small town in the district of Sedgemoor. The development will include a new primary school for 210 pupils, outdoor play facilities and public spaces. The site will also provide opportunities for new walkways and a cycle route into Highbridge.

Study the Ordnance Survey map extract of the Highbridge area; Diagram Q5A; Diagram Q5B; Diagram Q5C; and Diagram Q5D before answering this question.

Referring to evidence from the OS map extract and information from the other sources:

(a) **discuss** the suitability of the site, shown on Diagram Q5A, for the proposed housing development **and**

(b) **suggest** any social, economic or environmental impacts this development may have on the local area.   **20**

Diagram Q5A: Proposed site for new housing development in Highbridge, Sedgemoor district

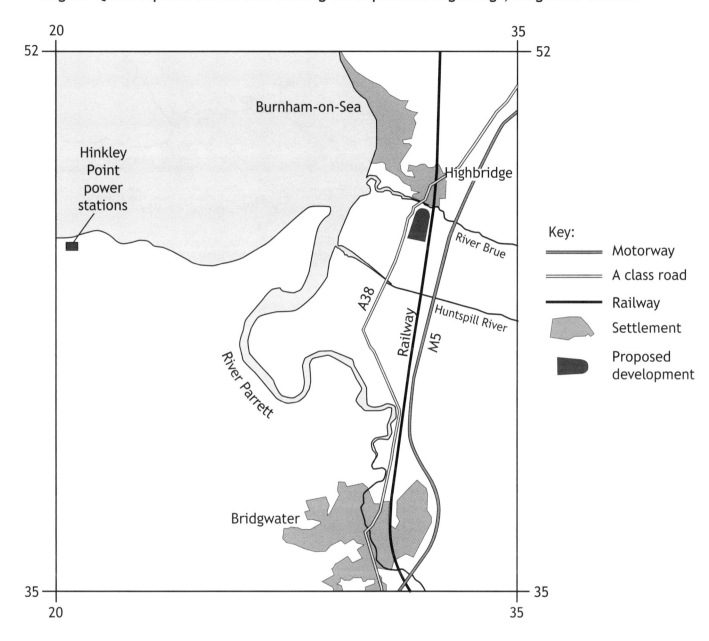

Diagram Q5B: Location of Highbridge

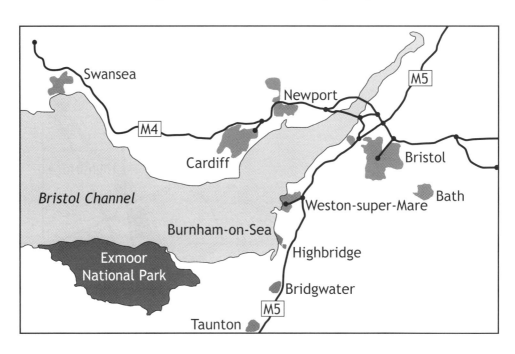

Diagram Q5C: Population of Sedgemoor district

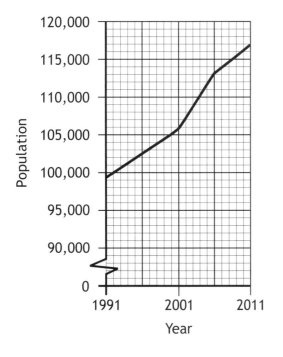

Diagram Q5D: News article from Yeovil Express, October 2015

YEOVIL EXPRESS

Hinkley Point C is good news for local area

The expansion of the nuclear power station will provide 25,000 new jobs to the area during construction. EDF Energy has also been busy putting into place the infrastructure that will help deliver the project and reduce its impact for the local community. £16 million has been invested in improving the local road network in Bridgwater and surrounding areas.

[END OF SPECIMEN QUESTION PAPER]

[BLANK PAGE]

DO NOT WRITE ON THIS PAGE

[BLANK PAGE]

DO NOT WRITE ON THIS PAGE

National
Qualifications
SPECIMEN ONLY

S833/76/22

Date — Not applicable

Duration — 1 hour 10 minutes

**Geography
Global Issues and
Geographical Skills
Ordnance Survey Map**

ORDNANCE SURVEY MAP

For Question 5

Note: The colours used in the printing of this map extract are indicated in the four little boxes at the top of the map extract. Each box should contain a colour; if any does not, the map is incomplete and should be returned to the Invigilator.

Ordnance
Survey

ROADS AND PATHS

Not necessarily rights of way

Junction number
Service area   Elevated
M1
Unfenced

Motorway (dual carriageway)

A 470   Dual carriageway

A 493   Footbridge

Primary Route
(A network of recommended through routes
which complement the motorway system)

Main road

Road under construction

B 4518

Secondary road

A 855   Bridge   B 885

Narrow road with passing places

Road generally more than 4m wide

Road generally less than 4m wide

Path / Other road, drive or track

Gradient: steeper than 20% (1 in 5),
14% to 20% (1 in 7 to 1 in 5)

Gates, Road tunnel

Ferry P   Ferry V

Ferry (passenger), Ferry (vehicle)

RAILWAYS

Track multiple or single

Track under construction

Siding

Tunnel, cuttings

Narrow gauge, tramway
or light rail system

Bridges, footbridge

Level crossing

Viaduct, embankment

Station, (a) principal

Light rail station

WATER FEATURES

Marsh or salting

Towpath   Lock

Aqueduct   Canal   Ford

Weir

Lake   Footbridge   Bridge

Canal (dry)

Slopes   Cliff

Flat rock

Beacon

Sand   Lighthouse
Dunes   (disused)

Normal tidal limit

Shingle

Lighthouse
(in use)

Low water mark

Mud

High water mark

HEIGHTS

1 metre = 3·2808 feet

Contours are at 10 metres
vertical interval

·144

Heights are to the nearest
metre above mean sea level

Where two heights are shown, the first is
the height of the natural ground in the
location of the triangulation pillar, and the
second (in brackets) to a separate point
which is the natural summit.

ROCK FEATURES

Outcrop

Cliff

Scree

PUBLIC RIGHTS OF WAY

Footpath

Bridleway

Restricted byway (not for
use by mechanically
propelled vehicles)

Byway open to all traffic

The symbols show the defined route so far
as the scale of mapping will allow.

The representation on this map of any other
road, track or path is no evidence of the
existence of a right of way. Not shown on
maps of Scotland

Danger Area

Firing and Test Ranges
in the area. Danger!
Observe warning notices.

OTHER PUBLIC ACCESS

Other route with public access
(not normally shown in urban
areas). Alignments are based on
the best information available.
These routes are not shown on
maps of Scotland.

On-road cycle route

Traffic-free cycle route

4   National Cycle Network number

8   Regional Cycle Network number

National Trail, Scotland's Great Trails,
European Long Distance Path and
selected Recreational Routes

TOURIST INFORMATION

Camp site / caravan site

Garden/aboretum

Golf course or links

Information centre (all year / seasonal)

Nature reserve

Parking, Park and ride (all year / seasonal)

Picnic site

Recreation / leisure / sports centre

Selected places of tourist interest

Phone, public / emergency

Viewpoint

V   Visitor centre

Walks / Trails

World Heritage site or area

Youth hostel

LAND FEATURES

Electricity transmission line
(pylons shown at standard spacing)

Pipe line
(arrow indicates direction of flow)

ruin   Buildings

Important building (selected)

Bus or coach station

Current or   with tower
former place
of worship   with spire, minaret or dome

+   Place of worship

Glass structure

H   Heliport

Triangulation pillar

Mast

Wind pump

Wind turbine

Windmill with or without sails

Graticule intersection at 5' intervals

Cutting, embankment

Landfill site or slag/spoil heap

Coniferous wood

Non-coniferous wood

Mixed wood

Orchard

Park or ornamental ground

Forestry Commission land

National Trust (always open / limited access,
observe local signs)

Natural Resources Wales

National Trust for Scotland (always open /
limited access, observe local signs)

BOUNDARIES

National

District

County, Unitary Authority,
Metropolitan District
or London Borough

National Park

ANTIQUITIES

+   Site of antiquity

Site of Battle (with date)

Visible earthwork

VILLA   Roman

Castle   Non-Roman

ABBREVIATIONS

Br	Bridge	MS	Milestone
Cemy	Cemetery	Mus	Museum
CG	Cattle grid	P	Post office
CH	Clubhouse	PC	Public convenience (in rural areas)
Fm	Farm	PH	Public house
Hospl	Hospital	Sch	School
Ho	House	TH	Town Hall, Guildhall or equivalent
MP	Milepost	Univ	University

Scale 1: 50 000

2 centimetres to 1 kilometre (one grid square)

2   1   0 Kilometres   1   2   3

1   0 Miles   1   2

1 kilometre = 0·6214 mile

1 mile = 1·6093 kilometres

Magnetic North   Grid North   True North

Diagrammatic only

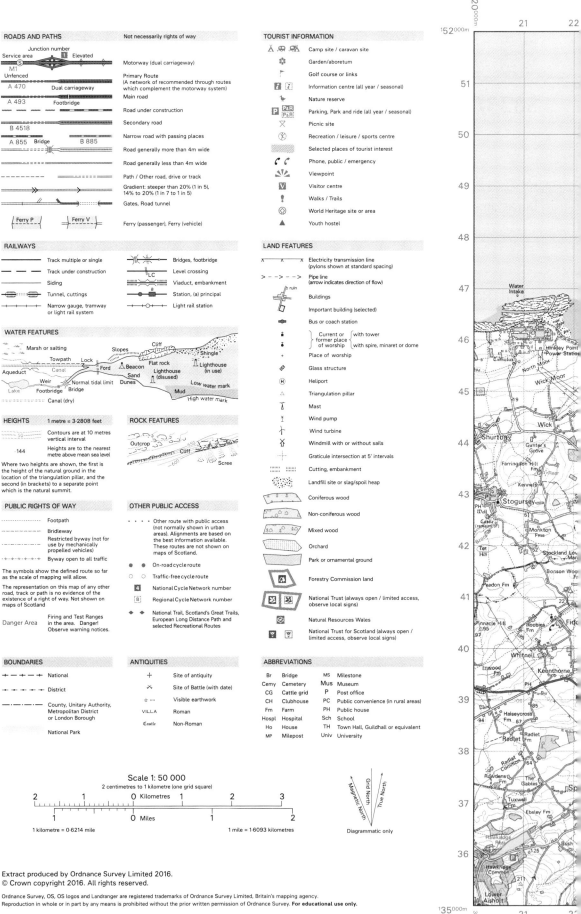

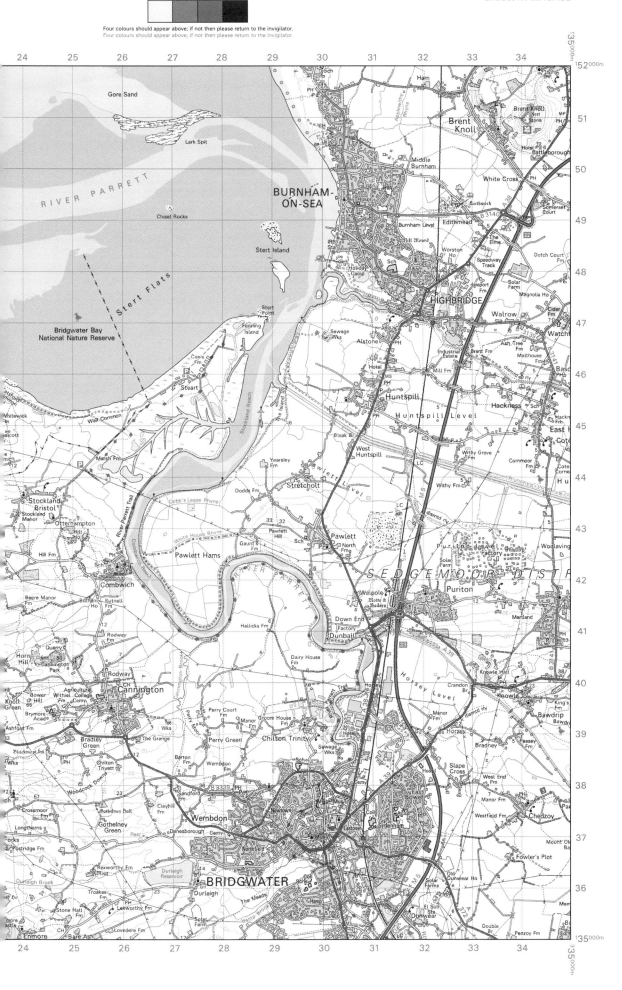

Four colours should appear above; if not then please return to the invigilator.
Four colours should appear above; if not then please return to the invigilator.

135 000m
152 000m

24 25 26 27 28 29 30 31 32 33 34

Gore Sand

Lark Spit

RIVER PARRETT

Chisel Rocks

Stert Island

BURNHAM-
ON-SEA

Brent
Knoll

Battleborough

Middle
Burnham

White Cross

Somerset
Court

Earthwork

Burnham Level

Edithmead

B 3140

The
Elms

Dutch Court
Fm

Worston
Ho

Solar
Farm

Magnolia Ho

HIGHBRIDGE

Walrow

Cider
Fm

Watchfield

Stert Flats

Stert
Point

Fenning
Island

Sewage
Wks

Holiday
Camp

Alstone

Ash Tree
Fm

Brent Fm

Malthouse
Fm

Industrial
Estate

Basor

Bridgwater Bay
National Nature Reserve

Steart

Coxs Fm

Hotel

Mill Fm

Huntspill

Hackness

Stockland Reach

Wall Common

Marsh Fm

Yearsley
Fm

Bleak Br

West
Huntspill

Huntspill Level

Withy Grove

Commoor
Fm

East

Cote
Corner

The Island

Stretcholt

Dodde Fm

Withy Fm

Stockland
Bristol

Stockland
Manor

Otterhampton

Cobb's Leaze Rhyne

River Parrett Trail

White House Rhyne

Pawlett Hams

Gaunt's
Fm

Pawlett
Hill

Pawlett

North
Fm

SEDGEMOOR DIST

Purtington

Factory

Puriton

Solar
Farm

Woolaving

Combwich

Hill Fm

Hill
Fm

Sch

PH

RIVER PARRETT

Hallicks Fm

Down End

Factory

Dunball

Walpole

Motte &
Bailey

Martland

Beere Manor
Fm

Botham
Ho

Putnell
Fm

Rodway
Fm

Quarry

Dairy House
Fm

Horsey Level

Knowle Hall

Horn
Hill

Cannington
Park

Rodway

Agricultural
Withiel
Fm

College

Cannington

Cemy

Perry Court
Fm

Manor
Fm

Groom House
Fm

Manor
Fm

Crandon
Br

Knowle

King's
Cliff

Bawdrip

Bower
Hill

Brymore
Acad

Knoll
Green

Perry Moor

Perry Green

Chilton Trinity

Sewage
Wks

Horsey

Peasey
Fm

Slape
Cross

West End
Fm

Manor Fm

Ashford Fm

Bradley
Green

The Grange

Barton
Fm

Wembdon

School

Bradney

Chedzoy

Par

Blackmore Hill

Wks

Chilton
Trivett

Woodcock Downs

Sandford

Clayhill

B 3339

Newtown

Coll

Sidenham

Westfield
Fm

Crossmoor

Gothelney Hall

Wembdon

Danesborough

Cemy

Northfield

Eastover

Fowler's Plot

Mount
Ba

Longthorns

Gothelney
Green

Rexworthy Fm

Durleigh
Reservoir

Dunwear Ho

Old
Dunwear

Solar
Farms

Postridge Fm

Durleigh Brook

BRIDGWATER

Durleigh

The Meads

El Sub
Sta

Dunwear

Double
Br

Penzoy Fm

Troakes
Fm

Stone Hall
Fm

Lexworthy Fm

Lovedere Fm

Solar
Farm

Bare Ash

Enmore

135 000m
135 000m

24 25 26 27 28 29 30 31 32 33 34

[BLANK PAGE]

DO NOT WRITE ON THIS PAGE

HIGHER

Answers

General Marking Principles for Higher Geography

This information is provided to help you understand the general principles you must apply when marking candidate responses to questions in this Paper. These principles must be read in conjunction with the detailed marking instructions, which identify the key features required in candidate responses.

a) Marks for each candidate response must always be assigned in line with these General Marking Principles and the Detailed Marking Instructions for this assessment.

b) Marking should always be positive. This means that, for each candidate response, marks are accumulated for the demonstration of relevant skills, knowledge and understanding: they are not deducted from a maximum on the basis of errors or omissions.

c) Where the candidate violates the rubric of the paper and answers two parts in one section, both responses should be marked and the better mark recorded.

d) Marking must be consistent. Never make a hasty judgement on a response based on length, quality of hand writing or a confused start.

e) Use the full range of marks available for each question.

f) The Detailed Marking Instructions are not an exhaustive list. Other relevant points should be credited.

g) For credit to be given, points must relate to the question asked. Where candidates give points of knowledge without specifying the context, these should be rewarded unless it is clear that they do not refer to the context of the question.

h) For knowledge/understanding marks to be awarded, points must be:
   a. relevant to the issue in the question
   b. developed (by providing additional detail, exemplification, reasons or evidence)
   c. used to respond to the demands of the question (ie evaluate, analyse, etc)

Marking principles for each question type

There are a range of types of question which could be asked within this question paper. For each, the following provides an overview of marking principles, and an example for each.

Explain

Questions which ask candidates to explain or suggest reasons for the cause or impact of something, or require them to refer to causal connections and relationships: candidates must do more than describe to gain credit here.

Where this occurs in a question asking about a landscape feature, candidates should refer to the processes leading to landscape formation.

Where candidates are provided with sources, they should make use of these and refer to them within their answer for full marks.

Where candidates provide a purely descriptive answer, or one where development is limited, no more than half marks should be awarded for the question.

Other questions look for higher-order skills to be demonstrated and will use command words such as analyse, evaluate, to what extent does, discuss.

Analyse

Analysis involves identifying parts, the relationship between them, and their relationships with the whole. It can also involve drawing out and relating implications.

An analysis mark should be awarded where a candidate uses their knowledge and understanding/a source, to identify relevant components (eg of an idea, theory, argument, etc) and clearly show at least one of the following:

- links between different components
- links between component(s) and the whole
- links between component(s) and related concepts
- similarities and contradictions
- consistency and inconsistency
- different views/interpretations
- possible consequences/implications
- the relative importance of components
- understanding of underlying order or structure

Where candidates are asked to analyse they should identify parts of a topic or issue and refer to the interrelationships between, or impacts of, various factors, eg analyse the soil-forming properties which lead to the formation of a gley soil. Candidates would be expected to refer to how the various soil formatting properties contributed to the formation.

Evaluate

Where candidates are asked to evaluate, they should be making a judgement of the success, failure, or impact of something based on criteria. Candidates would be expected to briefly describe the strategy/project being evaluated before offering an evidenced conclusion.

Account for

Where candidates are being asked to account for, they are required to give reasons, often (but not exclusively) from a resource, eg for a change in trade figures, a need for water management, or differences in development between contrasting developing countries.

Discuss

These questions are looking for candidates to explore ideas about a project, or the impact of a change. Candidates will be expected to consider different views on an issue/argument. This might not be a balanced argument, but there should be a range of impacts or ideas within the answer.

To what extent

This asks candidates to consider the impact of a management strategy or strategies they have explored. Candidates would be expected to briefly describe the strategy/project being evaluated before offering an evidenced conclusion. Candidates do not need to offer an overall opinion based on a variety of strategies, but should assess each separately.

General Marking Information for students

When answering a question, you should ensure that you read the question carefully before you start. You should look at the command word to ensure you answer the question correctly, eg if the question asks you to explain, then you must give reasons to support your response. Remember that there are no describe questions so, if your answers do not contain more than a descriptive point, it will be difficult to achieve any marks. If a question asks for two points of view to be covered, for example, advantages and disadvantages, then both must be covered for full marks. If the question is out of six and only the advantages are covered, then a maximum mark of four or five might be awarded. If a named area or example is asked for, then you may lose a mark(s) if you give a general response to the question. There are often more points covered (worth a mark each) in the following answers than will be required. For example, there could be six or seven points listed for a five-mark answer. Since the question is only worth five marks then any five of the six points could gain the five marks.

HIGHER GEOGRAPHY
2016

Section 1: Physical Environments

Question			General marking principle for this type of question	Max mark	Specific marking instructions for this question
1.	(a) (b)		1 mark should be awarded for each developed comparison, or two limited comparisons up to a maximum of 3 marks. For full marks, candidates must answer both parts of the question. Award **1 mark for each detailed explanation or for two limited explanations.** Candidates may choose to answer this question holistically and should be credited accordingly. Award 1 mark for a limited comparison with a limited explanation. Credit any other valid responses	5	**Comparison** should highlight the marked contrast in precipitation totals, seasonal distribution and number of rain days. Figures may provide detail for a comparison, however they are not required. *Answers may include:* Agadez has 200mm rainfall compared with Lagos 1600mm. Agadez has a peak in August, whereas at Lagos there is a higher peak June. **(1 mark)** Agadez has a distinct dry season from October to May with one peak, whereas Lagos has year round rainfall with 2 peaks. **(1 mark)** **Explanation** should focus on explaining the migration of the ITCZ and the movement of the Maritime Tropical and Continental Tropical air masses over the course of the year. *Answers may include:* Lagos sits south of the ITCZ and is influenced by hot, humid maritime tropical air from the Gulf of Guinea for most of the year **(1 mark)**. The twin precipitation peaks can be attributed to the ITCZ moving northwards in the early part of the year and then southwards later in the year in line with thermal equator/overhead sun **(1 mark)**. Agadez, on the other hand, is under the influence of hot, dry continental tropical air blowing from the Sahara and lies well to the north of the ITCZ for most of the year **(1 mark)**.
2.	(a)		1 mark should be awarded for each developed explanation, or for two limited descriptions/explanations. If candidates discuss more than one glaciated area, mark all and award marks to the highest scoring section. If candidates discuss a coastal area, bracket the name off, and award marks to any conflict/ strategy which could apply to a glaciated area. Bracket off responses referring to social/ economic conflicts, although be aware that candidates may develop this by referring to economic consequences. Credit any other valid responses.	5	Precise points will depend on the conflict and area chosen (although the extracts refers to tourism, note that the question is open to all environmental conflicts). Traffic congestion on narrow rural roads leads to high levels of air and noise pollution **(1 mark)**. Tourists parking on grass verges in honeypot locations such as Bowness can lead to erosion of fragile grass verges **(1 mark)**. Tourists wander off footpaths widening them and stone wall can be damaged by people climbing over them **(1 mark)**. Litter causes visual pollution and can harm wildlife (or livestock) if it is eaten **(1 mark)**. Speedboats on lakes produce oil pollution and can erode beaches **(1 mark)**. Quarrying such as Honister Quarry in the Lake District can produce large quantities of dust which can settle on plants stunting their growth **(1 mark)**. Large lorries travelling to and from the quarries can cause structural damage due to vibrations from the heavily loaded vehicles **(1 mark)**.

Question			General marking principle for this type of question	Max mark	Specific marking instructions for this question
	(b)	(i) (ii)	1 mark should be awarded for each developed explanation and each developed evaluation, or for two limited descriptions/explanations/evaluations. Award 1 mark for a limited explanation with a limited evaluation. Candidates should be awarded a maximum of 4 marks if there is no evaluation. Candidates may choose to answer this question holistically and should be credited accordingly.	5	Removing litter bins in remote areas where it is difficult to empty them (leading to overflowing bins), encourages people to take their litter home **(1 mark)**. Traffic restrictions such as one way streets and limited waiting times have had limited success as people prefer the convenience of their own vehicles **(1 mark)**. Using farmers' fields as temporary car parks reduces on-street parking and can bring in another form of income for the farmer **(1 mark)**. Hosing lorries or covering with tarpaulin has reduced the amount of dust, and transporting by train takes lorries off the road **(1 mark)**. Planting trees around unsightly developments can shield them, but this is a long term solution **(1 mark)**. New developments are controlled by NPA by-laws ensuring they use local materials which blend in with the landscape **(1 mark)**. Speed limits to reduce beach erosion have been implemented, however, this has resulted in speedboat users moving to other lakes **(1 mark)**.

Section 2: Human Environments

Question		General marking principle for this type of question	Max mark	Specific marking instructions for this question
3.	(a) (b)	Answers will depend on the case study referenced by the candidate. For full marks candidates must answer both parts of the question. Marks may be awarded as follows: For 1 mark, candidates may give one detailed explanation, or a limited description/explanation of two factors. For 1 mark, candidates may give a developed comment on effectiveness or two limited comments on effectiveness. For 1 mark, candidates may give one limited explanation with one limited comment on effectiveness. Candidate responses are likely to address the question holistically and marks should be awarded accordingly. Credit any other valid responses.	6	*Suitable methods for Africa might include:* • Afforestation projects reduce wind erosion and prevent soil erosion as the tree roots bind the soil and hold it in place **(1 mark)**. • However, the current and anticipated cost of the Great Green Wall project has been heavily criticised; it is out of the reach of most developing nations **(1 mark)**. • Fanya juu terraces (popular in Makanya in north-eastern Tanzania) have been made by digging a drainage channel and throwing soil uphill to make a ridge to increase infiltration **(1 mark)**. • This low technology approach has been particularly successful. However, maintaining the terraces is very labour intensive **(1 mark)**. • In Makanya, maize is grown between the trenches increasing crop yield (from 1.5 tonnes per hectare to 2.4 tonnes per hectare) which reduces the need to cultivate more marginal farmland **(1 mark)**. • Diguettes or "Magic Stones" are lines of stones placed along the contours of gently sloping land to trap rain water as well as soil **(1 mark)**. • This is particularly useful following the seasonal rainfall in the Sahel caused by the ITCZ which causes surface run-off **(1 mark)**. • By preserving the most fertile top-soil, stone lines have increased yields by 40% in some areas **(1 mark)**.

Question		General marking principle for this type of question	Max mark	Specific marking instructions for this question
		(continued)		• Zai (microbasins, or planting pits) are hollows dug to retain moisture and nutrients **(1 mark)**. • This ensures year round plant coverage which increases infiltration and reduced run-off **(1 mark)**. *Other methods may include:* • Microdams • Education programmes • Managed grazing/moveable fencing *NB Suitable methods for a rainforest area may include:* • Re afforestation • Increased global co-operation • Crop rotation • Agroforestry • National Parks
4.	(a)	For 1 mark, candidates may give one detailed explanation, or a limited description/explanation of two factors. Credit any other valid responses.	3	*Population data can be gathered by:* • Census is a survey carried out every ten years to gather population data **(1 mark)**. • Census: Each householder is asked to complete a detailed questionnaire about the number of people living in their home, their age, gender, employment, home and languages spoken **(1 mark)**. • Civil registrations of births, marriages and deaths keep an up-to-date count of the population **(1 mark)**. • Sampling: Population surveys are conducted to gather social and economic data, and can be conducted at regional, national or international levels **(1 mark)**. • In China National Population Sample Surveys have been conducted annually, with 1% of the population being asked to complete the form **(1 mark)**. • Government records: Information on migration may be gathered from visa applications or Borders Agency **(1 mark)**. • Data from electoral roll and NHS records allows population data to be updated in between census collection **(1 mark)**.
	(b)	Candidates must explain the problems of collecting accurate population data in developing countries. For 1 mark, candidates may give one detailed explanation, or a limited explanation of two factors. Named examples will enhance a candidate's answer, however, a name alone will not gain any credit. Credit any other valid responses.	6	*Problems of gathering population data:* • Language barriers: countries with many official languages have to translate their census forms and employ enumerators who can speak multiple languages **(1 mark)**. • Literacy levels: many people can't read and write, and therefore are unable to complete the forms, or might make mistakes unintentionally **(1 mark)**. • Size of the population: the sheer size of some populations make it very difficult to conduct a census, eg in China and India **(1 mark)**. • Inaccessibility: the poor infrastructure and difficult terrain, for example in the Amazon Rainforest, may make it difficult for enumerators to distribute census forms **(1 mark)**. • Wars/civil wars: conflict can make it too dangerous for enumerators to enter, or for data to quickly become dated **(1 mark)**. • Cost: undertaking the census is a very expensive process, even for developed world countries. In developing countries, there may be higher priorities for spending, including housing, education and health care **(1 mark)**.

Question	General marking principle for this type of question	Max mark	Specific marking instructions for this question
	(continued)		• Migration: rapid rural to urban migration can make it difficult to gather accurate population data as data will become outdated very quickly **(1 mark)**. • Many people in developing countries may be living in shanty towns, eg Dhararvi, or are homeless, so have no official address making it difficult to count them **(1 mark)**. • People who are illegal immigrants are unlikely to complete a census for fear of deportation, leading to inaccurate data **(1 mark)**. • Nomadic people: large numbers of migrants, eg the Tuareg, Fulani or Bedouin, or shifting cultivators in the Amazon can easily be missed or counted twice **(1 mark)**. • Ethnic tensions and internal political rivalries may lead to inaccuracies, eg northern Nigeria was reported to have inflated its population figures to secure increased political representation **(1 mark)**.

Section 3: Global Issues

Question		General marking principle for this type of question	Max mark	Specific marking instructions for this question
5.	(a)	1 mark should be awarded for a detailed explanation or a limited description/ explanation of two factors; this may include the use of facts from the resources. Credit any other valid responses.	6	• Population increase of almost 50 million for country in last 20 years would require additional water for domestic use **(1 mark)**. • Irrigation is required for rice production to feed the population or for export **(1 mark)**. • Textile industries use large volumes of water therefore a reliable year round supply is required **(1 mark)**. • Due to the monsoon climate a lack of rainfall in Nov–March increases the need for water to be stored to allow use during the dry period **(1 mark)**. • The heavy monsoon rainfall of up to 800mm of rain in the month of July means there is a requirement to prevent flooding **(1 mark)**. • The city of Chittagong has a population of 7.5 million and is situated on the banks of the river; this increases the need for flood prevention **(1 mark)**. • Only 62% of the country has access to electricity, HEP from the dam could be used to improve this **(1 mark)**. • Excess energy produced could be exported to neighbouring countries such as India **(1 mark)**. • Improved sanitation means that far less of the population will be at risk from diseases such as cholera **(1 mark)**.
	(b)	Answers must discuss the possible positive **and** negative **environmental** impacts. Award a maximum of 3 marks for either. 1 mark should be awarded for a developed explanation, or a more straightforward explanation linked to the case study. Care should be taken not to credit purely social or economic benefits but markers should be aware that some candidates will be able to link these to the environment. Award a maximum of 3 marks if the answer is vague/does not relate to a specific named water management project.	4	*Answers will depend on the water management project chosen but for the Aswan High Dam, possible answers might include:* • Lake Nasser provides a sanctuary for waterfowl and wading birds and has more than 32 species of fish **(1 mark)**. • River and irrigation water becomes saline with high evaporation rates resulting in farmers downstream having to switch to more salt-tolerant crops **(1 mark)**. • The change in river regime has caused the loss of many animal habitats, eg the drying up of the Nile delta area may lead to inundation of sea water **(1 mark)**.

Question			General marking principle for this type of question	Max mark	Specific marking instructions for this question
	(b)		*(continued)*		• The water table is rising in the Nile valley, which is resulting in major erosion of foundations of ancient temples and monuments such as Abu Simbel **(1 mark)**. • Increase in 'clean' hydro-electric power from the 12 generating units in the Dam, instead of using polluting fossil fuels **(1 mark)**. • The lack of flooding and subsequent lack of silt deposition has led to a need for chemical fertilisers which has resulted in high levels of nitrogen and phosphorous being washed into rivers **(1 mark)**. • The sediments which were transported to the river mouth forming a delta are now trapped behind the dam, a situation which has led to severe erosion along the Egyptian coast **(1 mark)**.
6.	(a)		1 mark should be awarded for each detailed evaluation of the indicator, or for two more straightforward reasons. Candidates may respond by explaining the benefits of composite or other indicators. This should be credited accordingly.	3	• Single indicators such as GNI are averages which can hide extremes within a country such as a rich minority and a poor majority **(1 mark)**. • Development is not only about money, other aspects of development like literacy and health care are also important **(1 mark)**. • Composite indicators such as HDI give a more rounded picture; by combining a number of indicators **(1 mark)**. • It is not possible to tell where a rise in GNI is being spent within a country — not always spent on improving standard of living **(1 mark)**. • GNI is always expressed as US$ to allow comparison, however exchange rates continually fluctuate **(1 mark)**. • GNI does not take into account the informal economy however this accounts for a large proportion of wealth generated in some countries **(1 mark)**.
	(b)	(i) (ii)	1 mark should be awarded for each developed explanation or for two less developed explanations. A developed point may be: • a detailed explanation • a description of a strategy with a less detailed explanation • two less detailed explanations Evaluations may refer to why a strategy is suited to a developing country or by giving data to show how successful a programme has been. Answers which provide no evaluation should be awarded a maximum of 6 marks. Candidates may choose to answer holistically and should be credited accordingly. 1 mark should be awarded for a limited explanation with a limited evaluation. Candidate may discuss malaria in this question; only strategies which could be considered PHC should be credited.	7	• Oral Rehydration Therapy is the mixture of salt and sugar with clean water to help people suffering from diarrhoea **(1 mark)**; it is very effective as it is cheap and simple and it can be administered by untrained staff **(1 mark)**. • Vaccination programmes such as the UNICEF run polio immunisation campaign were delivered to rural areas as people here find it more difficult to access health care **(1 mark)**. • By 2014 polio was endemic in only three countries (Afghanistan, Pakistan and Nigeria) **(1 mark)**. • Charities such as Water Aid work with countries and other aid agencies to improve water and sanitation by installing, eg pit latrines **(1 mark)**. • By 2010 the number of people without access to improved drinking water had decreased to (11%) and the ash compost from latrines can improve crop yield **(1 mark)**. • Barefoot Doctors provide health education through play and songs as many people are illiterate in developing countries **(1 mark)**. • Insecticide treated bed nets provide a physical barrier against the mosquito and kills the mosquito preventing further spread **(1 mark)**. • However, they need to be treated regularly to be effective and in some cases are damaged by being used as fishing nets **(1 mark)**. • Play Pumps International provide roundabouts which extract ground water which can be used for drinking **(1 mark)**. These provide local people with transferable skills and use appropriate level of technology **(1 mark)**.

Question			General marking principle for this type of question	Max mark	Specific marking instructions for this question
7.	(a)		1 mark should be awarded for each detailed explanation or for a limited description/explanation of two factors. Markers should take care not to credit human causes of climate change. Credit any other valid responses.	4	*Possible answers might include:* • Milankovitch's theory: changes in the Earth's orbit and tilt alter the amount of energy reaching the Earth **(1 mark)**. • Every 41,000 years, there is a change in the tilt of the Earth's axis. A greater tilt means more sunlight in polar regions **(1 mark)**. • Over a 97,000 year cycle, the Earth's orbit stretches, affecting the amount of energy received **(1 mark)**. • Sunspot activity: global mean temperatures can be raised by peaks of sunspot activity, which follow an 11-year pattern **(1 mark)**. • Volcanic eruptions: after violent eruptions, large amounts of dust and droplets of sulphur may reflect the Sun's rays lowering temperature **(1 mark)**. • Retreating ice caps release additional fresh water leading to changes in oceanic circulation **(1 mark)**. • This also reduces the albedo effect as reflection has decreased as more land is exposed **(1 mark)**. • Melting permafrost: methane being released from melting permafrost from decomposing organic matter **(1 mark)**.
	(b)		For 1 mark, candidates should give one detailed explanation of the strategies used to manage climate change, or a limited description/explanation of two factors. Candidates do not need to refer to local, national and international strategies to gain full credit. Named examples will enhance a candidate's answer; however, an example alone will not gain any credit. Credit any other valid responses.		**Local—** • Individuals can reduce, re-use and recycle products so that less refuse is sent to landfill sites. This will reduce the amount of methane entering the atmosphere **(1 mark)**. • To reduce the amount of carbon dioxide generated by the burning of fossil fuels, households could reduce energy consumption by insulating their homes or switching lights off, etc. **(1 mark)**. • People could also be encouraged to use public transport, walk or cycle, or use hybrid or electric cars to cut down on fossil fuel consumption **(1 mark)**. • Fridge disposal should be managed carefully to ensure CFC gases don't escape. New cooling units no longer emit CFCs **(1 mark)**. **National—** • Government policies such as 'Helping Households to cut their Energy Bills' encourage the use of 'Smart Meters' improving energy efficiency **(1 mark)**. • Increasing the use of low carbon technologies such as windfarms: the UK Government is committed to creating 15% of energy by renewable sources **(1 mark)**. **International—** • The Paris Agreement outlined agreements between leaders of developed and developing countries to limit climate change below a 2° rise **(1 mark)**. • The European Union has committed to reducing carbon emissions by 20% by 2020. The EU will reward developing countries financially **(1 mark)**. • The impact of climate change could also be managed by preparing for extreme weather events, for example flood defences could be built to hold back flood water, or flood plains and natural wetlands could be used to store flood water **(1 mark)**.

Question			General marking principle for this type of question	Max mark	Specific marking instructions for this question
8.	(a)		1 mark should be awarded for each detailed comparison, or a comparison with a short explanation.	4	*Possible answers might include:*
			A detailed comparison will contain a qualitative statement such as dramatically higher and be supported by the statistics.		• Some countries can afford to buy in lots of imports (like USA who spend $2,273 billion) whereas other countries cannot afford to (like Zimbabwe who spend $4 billion) **(1 mark)**.
			A maximum of 2 marks should be awarded for answers which are purely descriptive and do not go beyond making comparisons directly from the table, with two such comparisons required for 1 mark.		• Some countries can sell manufactured goods to make money (for example, China who make $2,210 billion from exports), whereas other countries rely on raw materials (for example, Botswana who make $3 billion from exports) **(1 mark)**.
			Where candidates refer only to the headings (i.e. not to the data), a maximum of one mark should be awarded.		• China has the biggest trade surplus of $438 billion compared to the USA, which has the biggest trade deficit of $698 billion **(1 mark)**.
			Markers should take care to look for comparisons wherever they occur in a candidate's answer.		• Two countries with similar population sizes are Australia and Ghana, yet Australia has a trade surplus of $7 billion and a GDP per capita of $67,304, whereas Ghana has a trade deficit of $5 billion and a GDP per capita of $3,500 **(1 mark)**.
			Credit any other valid responses.		• Two countries with similar population sizes are China and India, yet China has a trade surplus of $438 billion and a GDP per capita of $6,071, whereas India has a trade deficit of $198 billion and a GDP per capita of $1,499 **(1 mark)**.
	(b)		1 mark should be awarded for each detailed explanation, or for two more straightforward explanations.	6	*Possible answers might include:*
			A maximum of 2 marks should be awarded for four straightforward descriptive lists, exemplified by country names.		• Some countries have the knowledge and technology to make and sell manufactured products, which sell at high prices and so larger profits are made **(1 mark)**.
			Take care not to credit the reverse points of answers with regards to primary/ manufactured products.		• These manufactured products sell for a more stable price so countries can plan for the future with confidence in future income **(1 mark)**.
			Credit any other valid responses.		• These primary products sell for prices that fluctuate, and so countries cannot invest in development for the future **(1 mark)**.
					• Often it is the 'developed countries', which set the price for primary products and keep them as low as possible by playing 'developing countries' against each other **(1 mark)**.
					• Some countries are too reliant on one or two low value exports, and so if anything happens to the price/production of these export products, the country's economy is hit badly **(1 mark)**.
					• For example, Saudi Arabia exports oil which is in high demand, whereas Burkina Faso exports shea nuts **(1 mark)**.
					• Trading blocs (like the EU) can control the trade terms for the benefit of its members and make it difficult for non-members to do as well **(1 mark)**. For example, they can set up tariffs and import duties that they charge non-member countries, which makes their goods appear less competitive **(1 mark)**.
					• They can also set quotas, which put a limit on the amount of product that a non-member country can sell to the member country **(1 mark)**.

Question			General marking principle for this type of question	Max mark	Specific marking instructions for this question
9.	(a)		1 mark should be awarded for each developed point or for two less developed points. A developed point may be a detailed explanation or a description of a trend with a less detailed explanation or may be two less detailed explanations. Credit any other valid responses.	5	• Increased vehicle ownership due to two-car households therefore increased demand for petrol (1 mark). • Increased ownership of electronic devices such as tablets, due to changing technology and affordability therefore increased demand for electricity (1 mark). • Increased standard of living and more single occupancy households leading to more houses with central heating systems (1 mark). • Improved energy efficiency in residential sector: for example, energy-saving fridges and LED lighting (1 mark). • Improved insulation of housing, such as cavity wall insulation cuts down on heat loss causing less heating to be required (1 mark). • Improved efficiency in cars and the growth of more affordable fuel efficient, 'greener' hybrid cars (1 mark). • Government initiatives, such as the cycle to work scheme encourage people to leave their cars at home by subsiding the cost of cycle purchase (1 mark). • The Government signed up to the Kyoto Protocol to reduce greenhouse gas emissions. This has led to targets for industry to meet in terms of energy savings (1 mark). • Significant dip around 2008 due to declining industrial output caused by the recession and subsequent lowering of manufacturing industry in the UK (1 mark).
	(b)		Award 1 mark for each developed advantage or disadvantage or for every two undeveloped points. Candidates must discuss advantages and disadvantages to gain full credit. Candidates must discuss a non-renewable source of energy. No marks for discussing renewable sources of energy. Candidates are expected to consider different aspects of their chosen source of energy. Credit any other valid responses.	5	*Possible answers for all non-renewable energy sources might include:* • They provide instant power as required meeting demand at peak times such as early evening (1 mark). • They cause air pollution and release greenhouse gases so contribute towards global warming (1 mark). *For 'fracking' other possible answers might include:* • The shale gas provides an alternative energy source reducing reliance on traditional fossil fuels such as oil which are finite (1 mark). • Noise and light pollution is increased due to 24hr production on shale gas sites (1 mark). • In USA shale gas production has allowed it to become self-sufficient in gas and means it does not have to rely on imports from other countries (1 mark). • However, the fracking fluid used in the process could pollute ground water and enter the domestic water system (1 mark). • The fracking process could be linked to causing minor earthquakes and tremors in the local area leading to structural damage to buildings and infrastructure (1 mark).

Section 4: Application of Geographical Skills

Question		General marking principle for this type of question	Max mark	Specific marking instructions for this question
10.	(a)	Candidates should make reference to all sources, including the OS map to discuss the suitability and impact of the by-pass route. It is possible that some points referred to as a disadvantage may be interpreted by other candidates as a negative impact. Markers should take care to credit each point only once, where it is best explained. 1 mark should be awarded where candidates refer to the resource and offer a brief explanation of its significance, or give a limited description/explanation of two factors. A maximum of 5 marks should be awarded for answers consisting solely of limited descriptive points with two such points required for 1 mark. A maximum of 4 marks should be awarded for candidates who give vague over-generalised answers, which make no reference to the map. There are a variety of ways for candidates to give map evidence including descriptions, grid references and place names. Credit any other valid responses.	10	*Possible advantages of this route:* • For the first 700m of the route at 745094, the road will be following a dismantled railway line. This will make the road easier to build here, and so reduce costs **(1 mark)**. *Possible disadvantages of this route:* • The new road will require several bridges to be built over rivers and the railway line (774113), which will increase the costs **(1 mark)**. • A road cutting required on approach to Upper Wilting farm as land rises steeply from Combe Haven may require more complex engineering works **(1 mark)**. • The new road crosses an area of marshland in square 7510, which will require costly drainage **(1 mark)**. • The new road is in the flood plain of Watermill Stream/Combe Haven, and so is at risk of flooding **(1 mark)**. *Possible impacts on the surrounding area might include:* **Negative Environmental Impacts** Diagram Q10C makes it clear that Sussex Wildlife Trust think the road will cause "unacceptable environmental damage". They might be referring to the fact that: • It will require the destruction of deciduous woodland at Chapel Wood and Park Wood (7711), which will cause habitat loss **(1 mark)**. • The road will spoil a natural landscape and cause visual pollution for walkers on the 1066 country walk **(1 mark)**. • The route passes close to sites of conservation value (SSSI, SNCI and an AONB), which could be spoiled by the amount of noise and air pollution a new road will bring **(1 mark)**. • The photograph shows street lighting following the new road which will cause light pollution to a rural area **(1 mark)**. **Positive Environmental Impacts** • Diagram Q10C shows that Glyne Gap is currently suffering from unsafe levels of air pollution on many days (sometimes as many as 16 days in a month), which the by-pass will reduce, improving the air quality here **(1 mark)**. • This will also reduce the noise pollution for local people in this area such as the suburbs of Bexhill, eg Pebsham **(1 mark)**. **Negative Socio-Economic Impacts** • The route passes through or very nearby several farms (Acton's Farm, Adam's Farm, Lower Wilting Farm for example), which could cause the disruption to the farmers as farm animals could be frightened by the noise of vehicles using the new road **(1 mark)**. • The route passes over several footpaths and bridleways including the "1066 Country Walk – Bexhill Link", which might be closed or at least spoiled by a busy new road **(1 mark)**. **Positive Socio-Economic Impacts** • Diagram Q10A shows that the A259 at Glyne Gap is currently very busy all day (with a peak flow of just under 2600 vehicles in an hour). The new road would reduce the traffic flow here dramatically, reducing traffic congestion **(1 mark)**. • This would save journey/commuting time and reduce transport costs for local people/businesses **(1 mark)**. • Building the new road will create many jobs and increase money for people in the local area, which will boost the economy **(1 mark)**.

HIGHER GEOGRAPHY
2018

Section 1: Physical Environments

Question	General marking instructions for this type of question	Max mark	Specific marking instructions for this question
1.	Award a **maximum of 3 marks** for any one element. Candidates should identify and discuss processes and their roles. A well annotated diagram could achieve **full marks**.	4	• input — precipitation mainly in the form of rainfall and snow, with the amount and duration having an impact on the level of water in the system **(1 mark)** • storage — on the surface in lakes and rivers and interception by leaves and roots of vegetation **(1 mark)**, with water also seeping into the ground, stored as soil moisture in the upper layers or deeper down in rock stores such as the water table **(1 mark)** • transfers — this includes the movement of clouds bearing moisture by the process of advection **(1 mark)** and surface run-off as sheet wash or rivers/tributaries, throughfall and/or stemflow, is responsible for the transferal of precipitation from the canopy to the soil **(1 mark)**, infiltration and/or percolation move water through the soil/rock **(1 mark)**. Throughflow is the movement of water through the upper soil layers towards the river, with the much slower groundwater flow taking longer to enter the river **(1 mark)** • output — evaporation, transpiration from vegetation and surface run-off from rivers into seas and oceans **(1 mark)**. **Or any other valid point.**
2.	Award a **maximum of 4 marks** for either feature. Check any diagram(s) for relevant points not present in the text and award accordingly. Well-annotated diagrams that explain conditions and processes can gain **full marks**. Award a **maximum of 1 mark** for three or more correctly named, but undeveloped, processes. Award a **maximum of 2 marks** for fully developed processes for any one feature. Answers which are purely descriptive, or have no mention of any processes or conditions, should achieve no more than **2 marks** in total, with **1 mark** being awarded for every two descriptive points being made.	7	**Erosional processes:** • erosion takes place due to hydraulic action — pounding waves compress trapped air in the rocks, creating an explosive blast which weakens and loosens rock fragments **(1 mark)** • abrasion/corrasion — rock fragments thrown against the headland create a sandblasting (abrasive) action, wearing away the rock **(1 mark)** • solution/corrosion — carbonic acid in sea water weathering limestone and chalk **(1 mark)** • attrition — rock fragments slowly being ground down by friction from wave action into smaller and rounder pieces to form sand **(1 mark)**. **Headland and bay:** • formed by differential erosion, where softer, less resistant rocks erodes more quickly than harder, resistant rocks **(1 mark)** • a headland is an area of hard rock which juts out into the sea and a bay is a sheltered area of softer rock between headlands **(1 mark)** • often form in areas with a discordant coastline where alternate bands of rock are found at right angles to the coast **(1 mark)** • constructive waves build a small beach in the sheltered bay between the headlands **(1 mark)**.

Question	General marking instructions for this type of question	Max mark	Specific marking instructions for this question
	(continued) **2 marks** The use of the names of at least two processes with development of these, but no other reference to conditions. Or limited use of the names of at least two processes, with at least two descriptive points about the landscape formation. **3 marks** Two developed processes with limited explanation of how the feature forms over time. **4 marks** Two named processes with development of these, with two further statements explaining the formation of the feature. If a candidate chooses a feature not in the question, award marks for relevant processes.		**Wave-cut platform:** • weaknesses such as joints, faults or cracks in cliffs are undercut by erosion to form a wave-cut notch **(1 mark)** • the rock above overhangs over the notch and, as erosion continues, the notch enlarges until the unsupported overhang collapses due to the weight **(1 mark)** • the new cliff face is then eroded and through time, the cliff retreats inland, leaving a gently-sloping rocky surface called a wave-cut platform, which extends out to sea away from the cliff **(1 mark)** • the platform is abraded by rock materials, with rock pools and pot holes forming, evident at low tide **(1 mark)**. **Or any other valid point.** **Depositional processes:** • both the deposition features are caused by the process of longshore drift, where waves, driven by the prevailing wind, push material up the beach; known as the swash **(1 mark)** • the returning backwash is dragged back by gravity down the beach at right angles **(1 mark)**. **Sand bar:** • formed when a spit grows across the entrance to a bay, connecting two headlands, enclosing a sheltered lagoon behind it **(1 mark)** • this happens when there is no strong flow of water from a river into the sea and through time, this stagnant lagoon water is infilled by deposition **(1 mark)** • bars form when there is a change in direction on a coastline, which allows a sheltered area for deposition **(1 mark)**. **Tombolo:** • formed when a spit extends out from the mainland, connecting to an island **(1 mark)**. **Or any other valid point.**
3.	'Explain' questions should make reference to causal relationships. Well-annotated diagrams that explain conditions and processes can gain **full marks.** Marks may be awarded as follows: For **1 mark**, candidates may give one detailed explanation. For **1 mark**, candidates may give a limited description with a limited explanation. A **maximum of 2 marks** should be awarded for answers consisting entirely of limited descriptive points, with two such points required for **1 mark**. Candidates may choose to answer by explaining and relating soil-forming factors or by referring to each horizon in the soil profile.	4	**Possible answers might include:** • natural vegetation – deciduous forest vegetation provides deep leaf litter, which is broken down rapidly in mild/warm climate **(1 mark)** • trees have long roots which penetrate deep into the soil, accessing nutrients from lower layers which are recycled to leaves **(1 mark)** • soil organisms – they ensure the mixing of the soil, aerating it and preventing the formation of distinct layers within the soil **(1 mark)** • climate – precipitation slightly exceeds evaporation, giving downward leaching of the most soluble minerals and the possibility of an iron pan forming, impeding drainage **(1 mark)**

Question	General marking instructions for this type of question	Max mark	Specific marking instructions for this question
	(continued)		• aspect — south-facing slopes in northern hemisphere with a greater amount of sunshine and higher temperatures increase the rate decomposition resulting in humus layer **(1 mark)** • rock type — determines the rate of weathering, with hard rocks such as schist taking longer to weather, producing thinner soils. Softer rocks, such as shale, weather more quickly **(1 mark)** • relief — tend to be found on gentler slopes leading to lower rates of erosions so thicker soils **(1 mark)**. **Or any other valid point.**

Section 2: Human Environments

Question	General marking instructions for this type of question	Max mark	Specific marking instructions for this question
4.	Answers will depend on the case study referenced by the candidate. Marks may be awarded as follows: For **1 mark**, candidates should briefly describe a strategy and offer one evaluative point. Further developed/detailed evaluative comments should be awarded **1 mark** each. At least two strategies are required for full credit. Up to **2 marks** can be awarded for description or explanation of strategies (ie no evaluation), with two such points required for **1 mark**. Credit any other valid responses.	5	**Large scale redevelopment:** • the Dharavi Redevelopment Project where local people will be moved to high rise apartment blocks, however, only those who have been resident in Dharavi since 2000 will be eligible to move into these apartments **(1 mark)** • other residents will be moved to other parts of the city, which will break up communities and may result in people being too far from their work **(1 mark)** • the new flats will also however be too small for those who currently have workshops above their homes **(1 mark)**. **Slum Rehabilitation:** • has planned and managed improvements such as upgrading mains sewerage to help reduce diseases such as cholera however, within twelve years, only 15% of Dharavi was redeveloped **(1 mark)**. **Local projects:** • self-help schemes support the efforts of local people to improve their housing for example by adding an additional floor to buildings thus reducing overcrowding **(1 mark)** • toilets have been added and are shared by two or three families who help to keep them clean, which has reduced the incidence of water related diseases **(1 mark)**. **Or any other valid point.**

Question			General marking instructions for this type of question	Max mark	Specific marking instructions for this question
5.			Candidates must explain the problems of collecting accurate population data in developing countries. For **1 mark**, candidates may give one detailed explanation, or a limited explanation of two factors.	6	**Problems of gathering population data:** • language barriers — countries with many official languages have to translate their census forms and employ enumerators who can speak multiple languages **(1 mark)** • literacy levels — many people can't read and write, and therefore are unable to complete the forms, or might make mistakes **(1 mark)** • size of the population — the sheer size of some populations make it very difficult to conduct a census, e.g. in China and India **(1 mark)** • inaccessibility — the poor infrastructure and difficult terrain, for example in the Amazon Rainforest, may make it difficult for enumerators to distribute census forms **(1 mark)** • wars/civil wars — conflict can make it too dangerous for enumerators to enter, or for data to quickly become dated **(1 mark)** • cost — undertaking the census is a very expensive process, even for developed world countries. In developing countries, there may be higher priorities for spending, including housing, education and health care **(1 mark)** • migration — rapid rural to urban migration, can make it difficult to gather accurate population data as data will become outdated very quickly **(1 mark)** • many people in developing countries may be living in shanty towns, e.g. Dhararvi, or are homeless, so have no official address making it difficult to count them **(1 mark)** • people who are illegal immigrants are unlikely to complete a census for fear of deportation, leading to inaccurate data **(1 mark)** • nomadic people — large numbers of migrants, e.g. the Tuareg or shifting cultivators in the Amazon can easily be missed or counted twice **(1 mark)** • ethnic tensions and internal political rivalries may lead to inaccuracies, e.g. northern Nigeria was reported to have inflated its population figures to secure increased political representation **(1 mark)**. **Or any other valid point.**

Question			General marking instructions for this type of question	Max mark	Specific marking instructions for this question
6.			Answers will depend on the case study referenced by the candidate. Marks may be awarded as follows: For **1 mark**, candidates may give one detailed explanation, or a limited description/ explanation of two strategies. A **maximum of 2 marks** should be awarded for answers consisting entirely of limited descriptive points, with two points required for **1 mark**.	4	**For rainforest areas:** • agro-forestry — farmers grow trees and crops at the same time to reduce large scale deforestation and subsequent soil erosion with protection from the rain/sun **(1 mark)** • the crops benefit from the nutrients from the dead organic matter decomposing adding to the fertility of soil **(1 mark)** • selective logging — trees are only felled when they reach a particular height. This allows young trees a guaranteed life span thus protecting the soil from erosion **(1 mark)** • afforestation projects reduce wind erosion and prevent soil erosion as the tree roots bind the soil and hold it in place **(1 mark)** • forest reserves — areas protected from exploitation, purchased by conservation groups or the government, allowing indigenous people to practice shifting cultivation which is less destructive of soil **(1 mark)** • monitoring — use of satellite technology and photography to check that any activities taking place are legal and follow guidelines for sustainability reduced deforestation by 60% in Brazil **(1 mark)**. **Suitable methods for a semi-arid area may include:** • afforestation projects reduce wind erosion and prevent soil erosion as the tree roots bind the soil and hold it in place **(1 mark)** • Fanya juu terraces (popular in Makanya in north-eastern Tanzania) have been made by digging a drainage channel and throwing soil uphill to make a ridge to increase infiltration **(1 mark)** • Diguettes or 'Magic Stones' are lines of stones placed along the contours of gently sloping land to trap rain water as well as soil **(1 mark)** • moveable fencing allows farmers to control grazing area allowing soil to recover at different times of the year **(1 mark)** • Zai (microbasins, or planting pits) are hollows dug to retain moisture and nutrients which increases infiltration/reduces run-off **(1 mark)**. **Or any other valid point.**

Section 3: Global Issues

Question			General marking instructions for this type of question	Max mark	Specific marking instructions for this question
7.	(a)		**1 mark** should be awarded for each detailed explanation. A **maximum of 2 marks** should be awarded for answers consisting entirely of limited descriptive points, with two points required for **1 mark**. Markers should take care not to credit physical factors. Although there could be overlap with factors like cost and cross-section, this must be clearly linked to human factors.	4	• to reduce construction costs for the dam a narrow cross section of the valley could be chosen **(1 mark)** • a site which is close to construction materials would help to reduce the cost of transporting these materials to the construction site **(1 mark)** • a site close to areas of farmland or urban areas would help to reduce water/electrical loss during transportation **(1 mark)** • an area of low population to reduce the costs for compensation and re-housing people who live in the area to be flooded **(1 mark)** • there is a need to be sensitive to native cultures for example many sites of archaeological importance in the Three Gorges Dam area were flooded or had to be relocated **(1 mark)**, or areas where there are important environmental considerations to avoid protests over concerns re the site of the dam • care has to be taken to avoid impacts on communication networks like road or rail links **(1 mark)** • workers will be needed therefore the distance to a nearby urban area to allow workers to commute easily needs to be considered **(1 mark)**. **Or any other valid point.**
	(b)		Award **1 mark** for each detailed explanation. For **full marks**, candidate answers must include both socio-economic and environmental benefits. No marks should be awarded for negative impacts. Award a **maximum of 5 marks** if the answer does not clearly relate to a specific named water management project. A **maximum of 3 marks** should be awarded for answers consisting entirely of limited descriptive points, with two such points required for **1 mark**.	6	**Answers will depend on the water management project chosen.** **For the Aswan High Dam, possible answers might include:** • increased access to clean drinking water reduces water borne diseases such as typhoid **(1 mark)** • increased irrigation, which allows for two crops a year to be grown, reducing malnutrition **(1 mark)** • production of wheat and sugar cane tripled allowing more export crops to be produced **(1 mark)** • increase in hydro-electric power attracting industries such as smelting industries **(1 mark)** • the introduction of the Nile perch and tiger fish into Lake Nasser has increased the income from commercial fishing industry and fishing tourism industry **(1 mark)** • industries which require large amounts of water have grown up near to Aswan, for example fertilisers, which creates jobs and generated foreign income **(1 mark)** • Lake Nasser provides a sanctuary for waterfowl and wading birds and has more than 32 species of fish **(1 mark)** • increase in 'clean' energy from the Dam, instead of using polluting fossil fuels reducing emissions which contribute to climate change **(1 mark)**. **Or any other valid point.**

Question			General marking instructions for this type of question	Max mark	Specific marking instructions for this question
8.	(a)		**1 mark** should be awarded for each detailed explanation, or for two more straightforward explanations. A **maximum of 2 marks** should be awarded for answers consisting entirely of limited descriptive points, with two points required for **1 mark**. Both positive and negative development factors can be awarded marks, but markers should take care to avoid crediting direct reversals.	5	• some countries such as Saudi Arabia have natural resources such as oil, which can be sold to generate foreign currency **(1 mark)** • some countries are landlocked and find it more expensive to export and import goods **(1 mark)** • a very hot and dry climate, which can cause desertification, makes it very difficult to grow crops to feed the population **(1 mark)** • some countries have beautiful beaches and scenery, which attracts tourists creating job opportunities **(1 mark)** • countries with a poor education system have many low skilled workers and are unable to attract foreign investment **(1 mark)** • corruption in government such as in Nigeria can lead to money being used inappropriately for military purposes **(1 mark)** • the lack of strict pollution laws in parts of SE Asia has also made some countries more attractive for manufacturing industries **(1 mark)** • where countries suffer from conflict or civil war they are unable to keep the economy working and spend extra finance on weapons **(1 mark)** • many countries suffer natural disasters which destroy infrastructure and wipe out efforts for development for example hurricanes in the Caribbean **(1 mark)** • countries which have accumulated large debts have to repay loans and interest causing less money for services **(1 mark)** • famine can lead to malnutrition, and a reduced capacity to work and create income **(1 mark)**. **Or any other valid point.**
	(b)		**1 mark** should be awarded for each description of a strategy with a limited evaluation. **1 mark** should be awarded for each developed evaluation or for two less developed evaluations. A **maximum of 2 marks** should be awarded for answers consisting entirely of limited descriptive points, with two points required for **1 mark**. Candidate may discuss malaria in this question however only strategies which could be considered PHC should be credited. A **maximum of 4 marks** can be awarded for any one strategy.	5	**Possible answers might include:** **Barefoot doctors** have been particularly effective because: • individuals were chosen by each village to be trained to a basic level of health care and so were fully trusted by the community **(1 mark)** • in countries with large rural areas it is very difficult to ensure that every village has access to a fully trained doctor/hospital **(1 mark)**. **The use of Oral Rehydration Therapy (ORT)** has been particularly effective because: • it is an easy, cheap and effective method of treating dehydration through diarrhoea — allowing even the poorest developing country to tackle this health problem **(1 mark)** • the World Health Organization estimates that ORT saves about 1 million babies each year in developing countries **(1 mark)**. **Organised Health Education Programmes** have been effective because: • they educate people about how to prevent diseases spreading for example by the use of mosquito nets to prevent malaria **(1 mark)**

Question			General marking instructions for this type of question	Max mark	Specific marking instructions for this question
			(continued)		• preventative healthcare such as vaccinations is easier and more cost-effective than trying to cure someone once they have a disease **(1 mark)** • the use of village meetings, songs, plays and posters to pass on health education messages are particularly effective in places with an illiterate population where a written leaflet would be of limited use **(1 mark)** • vaccination Programmes to immunise against preventable diseases like polio, cholera, measles, tetanus etc are estimated by the World Health Organization to save between 2 and 3 million lives every year **(1 mark)**. **Small-scale health projects** (such as pit latrines) can be effective because they: • use local labour and building materials for these projects reduces the cost and are readily available **(1 mark)** • they also provide the locals with training and transferable skills, which can help them to improve their standard of living in other ways **(1 mark)** • using local facilitators also ensures that the projects gain faster acceptance and usage in the local and wider community **(1 mark)**. **Or any other valid point.**
9.	(a)		For **1 mark**, candidates should give one detailed response, or a limited description of two factors. A **maximum of 3 marks** should be awarded for answers consisting entirely of limited descriptive points, with two such points required for **1 mark**. Candidates should be credited for both positive and negative impacts. Credit any other valid responses.	5	• sea level rises, caused by an expansion of the sea as it becomes warmer and also by the melting of glaciers and ice caps in Greenland, Antarctica, etc **(1 mark)** • low-lying coastal areas, e.g. Bangladesh, affected with large-scale displacement of people and loss of land for farming and destruction of property **(1 mark)** • more extreme and more variable weather, including floods, droughts, hurricanes and tornadoes becoming more frequent and intense **(1 mark)** • globally, an increase in precipitation, particularly in the winter in northern countries such as Scotland, but some areas like the USA Great Plains may experience drier conditions **(1 mark)** • increase in extent of tropical/vector borne diseases, e.g. yellow fever, as warmer areas expand, possibly up to 40 million more in Africa being exposed to risk of contracting malaria **(1 mark)** • longer growing seasons in many areas in northern Europe for example, increasing food production and range of crops being grown **(1 mark)** • habitat loss has largest impact on indigenous animals/plants, and in areas where migration to new habitats is more difficult, leading to estimates of 10% extinction rates for land species **(1 mark)** • increased sea temperatures have led to 80% coral bleaching. Extended periods of bleaching can kill the coral with knock on effects for other marine life **(1 mark)**

Question	General marking instructions for this type of question	Max mark	Specific marking instructions for this question
	(continued)		• changes to ocean current circulation, e.g. in the Atlantic the thermohaline circulation starts to lose impact on north-western Europe, resulting in considerably colder winters **(1 mark)** • changes in atmospheric patterns linking to changes in the monsoon caused by El Niño and La Niña **(1 mark)** • increased risk of forest fires, for example in Australia and California due to change in surface temperatures and changes in rainfall patterns **(1 mark)**. **Or any other valid point.**
(b)	For **1 mark**, candidates should give one detailed explanation of the strategies used to manage climate change, or a limited description/explanation of two strategies. Credit any other valid responses.	5	• individuals can reduce, reuse and recycle products so that less refuse is sent to landfill sites. This will reduce the amount of methane entering the atmosphere **(1 mark)** • to reduce the amount of carbon dioxide generated by the burning of fossil fuels, households could reduce energy consumption by insulating their homes or switching lights off **(1 mark)** • people could also be encouraged to use public transport, walk or cycle, or use hybrid or electric cars to cut down on fossil fuel consumption **(1 mark)** • fridge disposal should be managed carefully to ensure CFC gases don't escape. New cooling units no longer emit CFCs **(1 mark)** • Government Policies such as 'Helping Households to cut their Energy Bills' encourages the use of 'Smart Meters' improving energy efficiency by showing energy costs in pounds and pence **(1 mark)** • increasing the use of low carbon technologies such as windfarms — the UK Government is committed to creating 15% of energy by renewable sources by 2020 **(1 mark)** • UK government is committed to banning the sale of new petrol/diesel cars by 2040 to reduce emissions **(1 mark)** • the Paris agreement outlined agreements between leaders of developed and developing countries to limit climate change below a 2°C rise **(1 mark)** • the impact of climate change could also be managed by preparing for extreme weather events, for example, flood defences could be built to hold back flood water, or flood plains and natural wetlands could be used to store flood water **(1 mark)**. **Or any other valid point.**

Question			General marking instructions for this type of question	Max mark	Specific marking instructions for this question
10.	(a)		**1 mark** should be awarded for each detailed explanation or comparison. A **maximum of 2 marks** should be awarded for answers which are purely descriptive and do not go beyond making comparisons directly from the graph, with two such comparisons required for **1 mark**. Markers should take care to look for comparisons wherever they occur in a candidate's answer.	4	**Possible answers might include:** • developing countries such as those in Africa often sell primary products at low value, therefore profits are limited **(1 mark)** • developing countries in Africa are often disproportionally affected by natural disasters such as drought as they often rely on one or two primary goods **(1 mark)** • however, developed countries manufacture products, which adds value and provides increased profits **(1 mark)** • developing countries are deterred from exporting processed coffee as high import taxes would be placed on the coffee **(1 mark)** • patterns established during colonial times have been difficult to break which may account for the higher % of trade attributed to Europe **(1 mark)** • developed countries set the prices for raw materials through trading on commodity exchanges around the world, e.g. the New York Mercantile Exchange **(1 mark)** • many countries are unable to make a decent profit on the goods they sell because they are forced to pay tariffs to developed countries in trading blocs **(1 mark)**.
	(b)		**1 mark** should be awarded for each developed point. A developed point may be a detailed explanation, or a description with a less detailed explanation, or may be two less detailed explanations. For **full marks**, candidate answers must include both socio-economic and environmental benefits. Credit any other valid responses.	6	**Socio-economic impacts:** • people being trapped in poverty and trying to survive on very little money. This might be because companies in the developed world want to manufacture their product for the cheapest price possible **(1 mark)** • government subsidies and grants in developed countries allow companies to sell products (e.g rice and grain) at a cheaper price than is possible in many developing countries, undercutting local farmers and causing them to lose money **(1 mark)** • with little money they cannot afford things such as primary education for children. Many children are required to work to help the family earn a living instead of going to school **(1 mark)** • this causes an illiterate population, with the consequent lack of opportunities and poorer quality of living for people that this applies to **(1 mark)** • creates a cycle of poverty where the next generation are unable to access well paid employment due to being illiterate **(1 mark)** • the lack of well-paid jobs means many people live in shanty town type accommodation, with little access to clean water, safe electricity, sanitation etc **(1 mark)** • if a multinational company was to locate in a country this may improve the skills and education of local people increasing their standard of living **(1 mark)**. **Environmental Impacts:** • natural resources being over exploited which can lead to land degradation which can further reduce countries' ability to improve agriculture **(1 mark)**

Question			General marking instructions for this type of question	Max mark	Specific marking instructions for this question
			(continued)		• to the extraction of palm oil in Indonesia has resulted in damage to the environment. More than 40 million hectares of rainforest has been lost. **(1 mark)** • extracting resources leads to increased CO_2 emissions leading to an increase of greenhouse gases and global warming/climate change **(1 mark)**.
11.	(a)		**1 mark** should be awarded for each developed point for energy production or for two undeveloped points. A developed point may include a descriptive statistic/comparative statement with explanation or a developed explanation. Where candidates have only described the data, award a **maximum of 1 mark**. **1 mark** should be awarded for two descriptive points. Credit any other valid responses.	5	**Possible answers might include:** • Saudi Arabia is able to produce 569 million tonnes of oil a year due to vast natural resources of oil in its territory so it doesn't need to invest in other forms of energy **(1 mark)** • Brazil has the largest amount of Hydroelectric Power because it has large amounts of tropical precipitation and major rivers that can be harnessed **(1 mark)** • China and Brazil have invested heavily in large scale hydroelectric schemes in order to generate energy to prevent having to import oil and gas **(1 mark)** • the USA is able to produce large quantities of gas due to investment in techniques such as fracking which allows gas to be taken from deep underground **(1 mark)** • this allows the USA to export large quantities of gas but also it is consumed within the country so that it is not reliant on oil from other countries **(1 mark)** • Kazakhstan is able to produce large amounts of Nuclear power as it has large reservoirs of uranium, it has 12% of the world's reservoirs **(1 mark)** • Kazakhstan has electricity grid links to Russia, Kyrgyzstan and Uzbekistan and is also planning links to China, this means energy can be sold abroad to boost income **(1 mark)**.
	(b)		Award **1 mark** for each developed advantage or disadvantage or for every two undeveloped points. Candidates must discuss advantages and disadvantages to gain full credit. Candidates must discuss a non-renewable source of energy. No marks for discussing renewable sources of energy. Candidates are expected to consider different aspects of their chosen source of energy. Credit any other valid responses.	5	**Possible answers might include:** • non-renewable energy provides instant power as required meeting demand at peak times such as early evening **(1 mark)** • non-renewable energy can cause pollution and may release greenhouse gases so contribute towards global warming **(1 mark)**. **For 'fracking' other possible answers could include:** • the shale gas provides an alternative energy source reducing reliance on traditional fossil fuels, such as oil, which are finite **(1 mark)** • noise and light pollution is increased due to 24hr production on shale gas sites **(1 mark)** • in USA shale gas production has allowed it to become self-sufficient in gas and means it does not have to rely on imports from other countries **(1 mark)** • however, the fracking fluid used in the process could pollute ground water and enter the domestic water system **(1 mark)** • the fracking process could be linked to causing minor earthquakes and tremors in the local area leading to building damage **(1 mark)**.

Section 4: Application of Geographical Skills

Question			General marking instructions for this type of question	Max mark	Specific marking instructions for this question
12.			Candidates should make reference to all sources, including the OS map to discuss the impact of the High speed train line. **1 mark** should be awarded where candidates refer to the resource and offer a brief explanation of its significance, or give a limited description/explanation of two factors. A **maximum of 5 marks** should be awarded for answers consisting solely of limited descriptive points with two such points required for **1 mark**. A **maximum of 4 marks** should be awarded for candidates who give vague over-generalised answers, which make no reference to the map. There are a variety of ways for candidates to give map evidence including descriptions, grid references and place names. Credit any other valid responses.	10	**Advantages of Route:** • the HS2 line uses a section of disused railway in grid squares (2576 & 2577) which will reduce costs and disruption **(1 mark)** • the land is generally very flat thereby reducing costs while it is urbanised therefore reducing the visual impact **(1 mark)** • the route avoids areas of housing thereby reducing the impact on families and cost of relocation/compensation **(1 mark)**. **Disadvantages of Route:** • the route crosses many main roads and motorways such as the M6 & M42, this will increase the cost of the line as many bridges/tunnels will be required **(1 mark)** • the railway has to cross a number of waterways such as the River Blyth which will increase costs for drainage **(1 mark)**. **Positive Impacts:** • reduction in travel time from London to Birmingham will allow more business to take place between the two cities and will therefore increase jobs and the economy **(1 mark)** • the train line will create many jobs and generate money for the economy, by bringing in more international companies **(1 mark)** • Birmingham international airport will be able to do more business as it is connected to London via the high speed train line **(1 mark)** • the interchange train station is close to the national exhibition centre (NEC) which will allow more people to travel to the shows there and therefore encourage more trade and sales **(1 mark)** • however, the NEC is on the other side of the M42 which will make it difficult to get there from the train station **(1 mark)** • in future years phase 2 will link to Manchester and Leeds bringing even more business to the area **(1 mark)** • more expensive commuter areas like Balsall Common have far more concerns with over 160 in relation to noise pollution as this area is more rural **(1 mark)** • noise is less of a concern for the people of Chelsmey Wood — this may be because the area is next to the airport so the people are more used to the increased noise levels **(1 mark)**. **Negative Impacts:** • Birmingham international airport may lose passengers to the high speed railway as the journey time is cut and it takes passengers into the city centre **(1 mark)** • a large number of people, approx. 152 in the Hampton/Balsall area, are worried about the visual impact as the line travels through open area/countryside i.e. grid square (2181) **(1 mark)**

Question	General marking instructions for this type of question	Max mark	Specific marking instructions for this question
	(continued)		• the noise and vibrations from the line and it construction would be a negative particularly for people living in the more residential areas of Hampton in Arden and Balsall Common **(1 mark)** • a number of farms will lose land to the construction of the rail line having a negative impact on their ability to keep enough livestock/crops to be profitable **(1 mark)**, while other farms such as Pasture farm (208 828) will completely disappear meaning farmers losing their way of life **(1 mark)** • the biggest concern from those in Chelmsley Wood is in relation to transport and traffic as the line crosses a number of main road networks including the M6 and M42, the construction of the line would cause severe traffic issues as bridges or tunnels are constructed **(1 mark)**. **Or any other valid point.**

HIGHER GEOGRAPHY
2018 SPECIMEN QUESTION PAPER

Section 1: Physical Environments

Question			General marking instructions for this type of question	Max mark	Specific marking instructions for this question
1.			Check any diagram(s) for relevant points not present in the text and award marks accordingly. Award full marks for well-annotated diagrams that explain the formation of a meander. Award **a maximum of 2 marks** for a list of unexplained processes, with two processes required for each mark. Award **a maximum of 4 marks** for two fully developed processes (up to **2 marks** for each process). Award **0 marks** for the development of an ox-bow lake.	8	Meanders are formed by: • hydraulic action **(1 mark)** which is when air is compressed into the river bank causing materials to be dislodged **(1 mark)** • abrasion **(1 mark)** when the force of the water throws bedload against the banks causing erosion **(1 mark)** • riffles and pools lead to changes in speed and depths in the river channel **(1 mark)** • pools are areas of deeper water whereas riffles are shallower with greater turbulence **(2 marks)** • river flows fastest on the outside bend increasing the erosive power **(1 mark)** • river flows slowest on the inside bend leading to deposition **(1 mark)** • helicoidal flow moves materials across the river channel. **(1 mark)** This leads to river cliffs and beaches developing **(1 mark)** • meanders migrate downstream as erosion continues. **(1 mark)** **Or any other valid point.**
2.	(a) and (b)		Candidates must include both descriptions and explanation for full marks. Award **a maximum of 5 marks** for descriptions. Candidates may answer each command separately or as a holistic answer. Award marks accordingly.	10	Descriptions may include: • there is a lag time of five hours **(1 mark)** • there is a slow rise in discharge until 09:00 **(1 mark)** • there is a steep rising limb (1 mark) leading to a peak discharge of 100 cumecs at 18:00 **(1 mark)** • the rising limb becomes less steep briefly between 13:00 and 15:00 **(1 mark)** • there is a steep recession limb from 18:00 until 22:00. **(1 mark)**

Question	General marking instructions for this type of question	Max mark	Specific marking instructions for this question
	(continued)		Explanations may include: • this is caused by the initial rainfall which began at 07:00 **(1 mark)** • this rain may have been intercepted by vegetation **(1 mark)** • the water may also have infiltrated and be stored in the soil **(1 mark)** • the river rises because soil storage has been exceeded **(1 mark)** • the river may rise because of impermeable surfaces leading to rapid surface run-off **(2 marks)** • there may be a high number of tributaries transporting water to the channel quickly **(1 mark)** • it may be a small catchment area meaning less travel time to the main channel **(1 mark)** • the catchment area may be steep leading to rapid overland flow to the channel **(1 mark)** • the steep recession limb is due to there being no further rain after 15:00. **(1 mark)** Or any other valid point.
3.	Award **a maximum of 6 marks** if candidates do not provide an annotated profile. Award **a maximum of 6 marks** where candidates provide a 'ladder' type diagram (with A, B, and C horizons) and separate text answer.	8	 Associated vegetation is coniferous forest or heather moorland. **(1 mark)** Plants have shallow, spreading roots. **(1 mark)** Thin black humus layer. **(1 mark)** Mor/acidic humus. **(1 mark)** Some darker staining in upper A horizon from humus. **(1 mark)** Ash-grey lower A horizon **(1 mark)** with sandy texture. **(1 mark)** Fe and Al minerals deposited. **(1 mark)** Well-defined horizons. **(1 mark)** Few soil biota to mix soil. **(1 mark)** Iron pan develops in upper B horizon **(1 mark)** impeding drainage and causing waterlogging. **(1 mark)** B horizon is reddish-brown **(1 mark)** with denser texture due to downward leaching. **(1 mark)** C horizon is parent material, generally weathered rock **(1 mark)** or glacial or fluvio-glacial material. **(1 mark)** Or any other valid point.

Question			General marking instructions for this type of question	Max mark	Specific marking instructions for this question
4.			Check any diagram(s) for relevant points not present in the text and award marks accordingly. Candidates can gain full marks for well-annotated diagrams that explain the formation of a ribbon lake. Award **a maximum of 2 marks** where candidates provide a list of unexplained processes, with two processes required for each mark. Award **a maximum of 6 marks** where candidates provide three fully developed processes (up to **2 marks** per developed process). Award **a maximum of 2 marks** for the formation of a glacier.	10	Points may include: • glacier forms in a north-facing hollow **(1 mark)** • snow is compressed to form firn/neve **(1 mark)** • moves downhill due to weight and gravity **(1 mark)** • plucking **(1 mark)** occurs when ice freezes on to bedrock, pulling loose rocks away from the valley sides, making it steeper **(1 mark)** • abrasion **(1 mark)** when the angular rock embedded in the ice grinds the bedrock, making the valley deeper **(1 mark)** • frost shattering **(1 mark)** continues to steepen the sides of the valley, when water in cracks in the rock turns to ice when temperatures drop below freezing; expansion and contraction weakens the rock until fragments break off **(1 mark)** • former interlocking spurs may be cut off by glacier **(1 mark)** resulting in steep crags or truncated spurs **(1 mark)** • over time the valley becomes straightened, widened and deepened **(1 mark)** • ribbon lakes can form where softer bedrock is eroded more deeply than the surrounding area **(1 mark)** • ribbon lakes can form where a terminal or recessional moraine creates a dam **(1 mark)** • an example is Lake Windermere **(1 mark)** Or any other valid point.
5.	(a)		Award **a maximum of 3 marks** for each air mass. For each air mass, award **1 mark** where candidates provide the origin and **2 marks** for any weather characteristics. Do not award marks for origin over sea (x) or land (y).	6	Maritime Tropical (mT): • origin — Atlantic Ocean/Gulf of Guinea **(1 mark)** • weather characteristics — hot, **(1 mark)** unstable air **(1 mark)** with high humidity, **(1 mark)** high precipitation. **(1 mark)** Continental Tropical (cT): • origin — Sahara Desert **(1 mark)** • weather characteristics — hotter/very hot, **(1 mark)** low precipitation, **(1 mark)** and stable air **(1 mark)** with low humidity. **(1 mark)** Or any other valid point.
	(b)	(i) and (ii)	Award **a maximum of 5 marks** for either description or explanation. Award **1 description mark** for each comparison. Candidates should highlight the marked contrast in precipitation totals, seasonal distribution and number of rain days. Candidates may answer each command separately or as a holistic answer. Award marks accordingly.	8	Descriptions may include: • the north is very dry with a much wetter south **(1 mark)** (Nioro with only 305 mm, Abidjan with 1390 mm) **(1 mark)** • Ouagadougou has a clear wet season/dry season regime whereas Abidjan has year-round rainfall **(1 mark)** • Abidjan has a twin-peak regime whereas the other areas have only one peak **(1 mark)** • Abidjan's peak rainfall is in June, whereas this is later as you move north — August in Nioro **(1 mark)** • Abidjan has a peak of 350 mm whereas Nioro's is approximately 100 mm. **(1 mark)**

Question			General marking instructions for this type of question	Max mark	Specific marking instructions for this question
			(continued)		**Explanations** should focus on the role of the intertropical convergence zone (ITCZ) and the movement of the Maritime Tropical and Continental Tropical air masses over the course of the year. For example: • the ITCZ is an area of low pressure where the trade winds meet **(1 mark)** • a band of rainfall is created where the two air masses meet pushing the maritime air up, cooling and condensing to form clouds **(1 mark)** • the twin precipitation peaks can be attributed to the ITCZ moving northwards in the early part of the year and then southwards later in the year **(1 mark)** in line with the thermal equator/overhead sun **(1 mark)** • Abidjan on the coast is influenced by mT air for most of the year. **(1 mark)** Nioro, on the other hand, is under the influence of cT air for most of the year. **(1 mark)** Or any other valid point.

Section 2: Human Environments

Question			General marking instructions for this type of question	Max mark	Specific marking instructions for this question
6.	(a)		Award **1 mark** for each descriptive point.		Points may include: • lack of basic facilities such as schools, water **(1 mark)** • lack of public utilities such as sewerage or power **(1 mark)** • high incidence of disease **(1 mark)** • high rates of unemployment **(1 mark)** • unsightly dwellings made out of scrap materials **(1 mark)** • located on areas prone to flooding or landslides **(1 mark)** • often built without legal permission **(1 mark)** • overcrowded dwellings lead to lack of privacy/waste. **(1 mark)** Or any other valid point.
	(b)		Award **1 mark** for each explanatory point. Award **a maximum of 2 marks** where candidates give appropriate named examples within the chosen city. Award **a maximum of 6 marks** where candidates give generic answers which do not refer to a specific city.		For Mumbai, answers may refer to: • the Dharavi Redevelopment Project **(1 mark)** where local people will be moved to high-rise apartment blocks **(1 mark)** • these aim to replicate the streets and build-in working and open spaces **(1 mark)** • slum rehabilitation has planned and managed improvements such as upgrading mains sewerage **(1 mark)** to help reduce diseases such as cholera **(1 mark)** • self-help schemes support the efforts of local people to improve their housing, **(1 mark)** for example by adding an additional floor to buildings thus reducing overcrowding. **(1 mark)** For example, the NGO SPARC supports this **(1 mark)** • residents have been given legal rights to land **(1 mark)** • residents have been supplied with building materials to strengthen/make safe the housing. **(1 mark)** Or any other valid point.

Question			General marking instructions for this type of question	Max mark	Specific marking instructions for this question
7.			Award **1 mark** for each explanation of a strategy. Award **1 mark** for each evaluative comment. Award **a maximum of 2 marks** where candidates give appropriate named examples within the case study area. Award **a maximum of 6 marks** for either part of the question. Candidates may answer the question holistically; award marks accordingly.	10	For example, answers on the Lake District may include: • litter bins in remote areas are removed because it is difficult to empty them regularly. **(1 mark)** This has been found to encourage people to take their litter home **(1 mark)** • traffic restrictions such as one-way streets and limited waiting times have been introduced to encourage the flow of traffic. **(1 mark)** They have had limited success as people prefer the convenience of their own vehicles **(1 mark)** • farmers' fields can be used as temporary car parks to reduce on-street parking **(1 mark)** This is successful because farmers buy into the scheme due to increased income **(1 mark)** • planting trees around unsightly developments can shield them. **(1 mark)** However, trees take a long time to grow therefore this is not a short-term solution **(1 mark)** • fix the fells **(1 mark)** • pitching technique using local stone improves the aesthetic appeal and durability — local stone blends in with the landscape **(2 marks)** • speed limits have been imposed on water users to reduce wake, **(1 mark)** for example Windermere, **(1 mark)** however this has only served to move the users to other lakes in the area. **(1 mark)** Or any other valid point.
8.	(a)		Award **1 mark** for each relevant point.	6	Points may include: • census is a survey carried out every 10 years **(1 mark)** • each householder is asked to complete a detailed questionnaire about the number of people living in their home **(1 mark)** • householders answer other questions on their social, economic and cultural background **(1 mark)** • civil registration of births, deaths **(1 mark)** provides an up-to-date count between censuses **(1 mark)** • Scottish household survey is a continuous survey based on a random sample of the population **(2 marks)** • governments also collect data on migration, for example visa applications, and NHS records provide health data. **(2 marks)** Or any other valid point.
	(b)		Award **1 mark** for each relevant point. Award **a maximum of 2 marks** where candidates give appropriate named examples to develop a point.	12	Points may include: • countries with many official languages have to translate their census forms **(1 mark)** • countries have to employ enumerators who can speak multiple languages. **(1 mark)** Nigeria has six major languages and hundreds of unofficial languages **(1 mark)** • low literacy levels — people are unable to complete the forms **(1 mark)** • size of the population — the sheer size of some populations makes it very difficult to conduct a census **(1 mark)**

Question	General marking instructions for this type of question	Max mark	Specific marking instructions for this question
	(continued)		• inaccessibility makes some areas very difficult to reach within the time frame. (**1 mark**) For example, Indonesia has many islands spread over a large area (**1 mark**) • conflict can make it too dangerous for enumerators to enter (**1 mark**) • data can quickly become out-of-date due to the high death rate (**1 mark**) • cost — in developing countries, there may be higher priorities for spending, such as health care (**1 mark**) • many people in developing countries may be living in shanty towns so have no official address (**1 mark**) • ethnic tensions and internal political rivalries may lead to inaccuracies (**1 mark**) for example, northern Nigeria was reported to have inflated its population figures to secure increased political representation (**1 mark**) • illegal immigrants wish to avoid detection, (**1 mark**) for example Burmese migrants in Thailand (**1 mark**) • Nomadic people may be missed or counted twice as they cross international borders. (**1 mark**) Or any other valid point.
9.		Award **a maximum of 3 marks** for description. For full marks candidates must answer both parts of the question.	8	Descriptions may include: • 16—29 group may decrease in size by 3% (**1 mark**) • 30—44 age group may increase by 1% (**1 mark**) • 75+ age group may increase by 82% (**1 mark**) • 0—15 group may increase by 3% (**1 mark**) • vast increase in elderly over 60 (**1 mark**) • overall decrease in working age population. (**1 mark**) Consequences may include: • increased cost of pensions to the government (**1 mark**) • increased tax contributions for economically-active population (**1 mark**) • in-migration may need to be encouraged (**1 mark**) • the retirement age may need to be increased (**1 mark**) • more services for older people, such as care homes (**1 mark**) • there may be a lower unemployment rate in the future (**1 mark**) • slight increase in birth rate may lead to future increase in workforce. (**1 mark**) Or any other valid point.

Section 3: Global Issues

Question			General marking instructions for this type of question	Max mark	Specific marking instructions for this question
1.	(a)	(i) and (ii)	Award **1 mark** for each descriptive factor. Award **1 mark** for each explanation. Award **a maximum of 5 marks** for descriptive points. Do not award marks for human factors. Although there could be overlap with factors like cost, this must be clearly linked to the **physical** environment.	8	Points may include: • narrow and deep valleys **(1 mark)** can be dammed more efficiently and require less construction materials, reducing the overall cost of the project **(1 mark)** • narrow valleys also have a reduced surface area **(1 mark)** and combined with low temperatures **(1 mark)** they reduce water loss from evaporation **(1 mark)** • if the site has impermeable rock **(1 mark)** this would reduce water loss from the reservoir by percolation **(1 mark)** • a geologically-stable area away from earthquake zones/fault lines **(1 mark)** will reduce the risk of damage or failure of the dam **(1 mark)** • a high drainage density, **(1 mark)** or high rainfall **(1 mark)** will ensure that the reservoir will receive enough water to avoid transfer from adjacent drainage basins. **(1 mark)** Or any other valid point.
	(b)		Award **1 mark** for each consequence and award further marks where the candidate has developed this. Candidates must include both socio-economic and environmental adverse consequences. Award **a maximum of 10 marks** if only one is discussed. Award **2 marks** where candidates give specific named examples within the case study area, which develop the answer. Award **0 marks** where candidates give positive consequences. Award **a maximum of 10 marks** if the answer does not clearly relate to a specific named water management project.	12	For example the Three Gorges Dam, China. Socio-economic consequences could include: • the displacement of millions of people from the Yangtze river region **(1 mark)**; hundreds of towns and villages, such as Yunyang, **(1 mark)** were evacuated and later submerged **(1 mark)** • those forced to relocate were promised compensation for the value of their homes and land **(1 mark)** although this did not cover the cost of relocation, and some of the money was lost through corruption **(1 mark)** • compensation in some instances has been as little as the equivalent of £5 a month, **(1 mark)** and many claim they have received only half the land compensation they were promised **(1 mark)** • people have been forced to move to more expensive cities and towns **(1 mark)** • the displaced people are mainly farmers with little formal education. This makes it difficult for them to find jobs in the cities and towns **(1 mark)** • farmers remaining in the region have had to migrate northwards on to steeper mountain slopes. **(1 mark)** This increases soil erosion in this area. **(1 mark)** Environmental consequences: • construction of the dam has led to an increase in landslides in the area **(1 mark)** as a result of erosion caused by the increases and decreases in reservoir water **(1 mark)** • there are 300 species of fish in the Yangtze river. The dam has created a barrier in the river and fish are not able to travel upstream to spawn, so the populations of the species have decreased **(2 marks)** • the Chinese River Dolphin **(1 mark)** is at risk of extinction because the construction area covers a large part of this animal's habitat **(1 mark)**

Question	General marking instructions for this type of question	Max mark	Specific marking instructions for this question
	(continued)		• decreases in freshwater flow have meant that more saltwater is creeping up the Yangtze, **(1 mark)** endangering fish populations already threatened by overfishing. **(1 mark)** Or any other valid point.
2.	Candidates may choose to answer parts (a) and (b) separately or together. Award **a maximum of 15 marks** if candidates do not comment on effectiveness. Award marks once for each evaluation point. For example, candidates can gain marks only once for referring to cost. Do not award marks for reversals. Award up to **3 marks** where candidates give appropriate named examples which develop the answer.	20	Measures taken to eradicate the mosquitoes include: • one method used was to spray pesticides/insecticides in an attempt to kill the Anopheles mosquitoes. **(1 mark)** For example, DDT is sprayed on walls in homes **(1 mark)** • breeding genetically-modified sterile mosquitoes. **(1 mark)** These mosquitoes are unable to carry the parasite/mosquitoes give birth to predominantly male offspring **(1 mark)** • specially designed mosquito traps mimic animals and humans by emitting a small amount of carbon dioxide **(1 mark)** in order to lure the mosquitoes into the trap where they are killed **(1 mark)** • BTI bacteria artificially grown in coconuts. **(1 mark)** The fermented coconuts are broken open after a few days and thrown into the mosquito larvae-infested ponds. **(1 mark)** The larvae eat the bacteria and have their stomach lining destroyed **(1 mark)** • putting larvae-eating fish into stagnant ponds or padi fields, **(1 mark)** such as the muddy loach **(1 mark)** • flushing reservoirs every seven days **(1 mark)** as it takes longer than this period of time for the larvae to develop into adult mosquitoes **(1 mark)** • planting eucalyptus trees **(1 mark)** can help soak up excess moisture and reduce the amount of stagnant water **(1 mark)** • covering standing water and water storage cans, **(1 mark)** for example the Oxfam bucket, **(1 mark)** reduces the chances of mosquitoes breeding near to homes or villages. **(1 mark)** Measures taken to treat those suffering from malaria include: • medication to kill the parasite/prevent infection **(1 mark)** such as quinine/Chloroquine/Lariam/Malarone/Artemisia **(1 mark)** • trials have produced a vaccine (1) such as RTS,S **(1 mark)** which has now been recommended as being safe for use, as prevention is better than cure **(1 mark)** • education programmes **(1 mark)** such as the WHO's 'Roll Back Malaria' campaign. **(1 mark)** In particular, educating people in the use of insect repellents **(1 mark)** or covering the skin at dawn/dusk **(1 mark)** when mosquitoes are most active, to reduce the chances of being bitten **(1 mark)** • the increased use of insecticide-coated mosquito nets at night. **(1 mark)**

Question	General marking instructions for this type of question	Max mark	Specific marking instructions for this question
(continued)			Possible comments on the effectiveness might include: • insecticides to kill the mosquito were effective at first, however the mosquito became resistant to DDT **(1 mark)** and alternative insecticides are often too expensive for developing countries **(1 mark)** • mosquito traps have been effective on a small scale **(1 mark)** • the BTI bacteria in coconuts is an environmentally-friendly solution, **(1 mark)** with two to three coconuts clearing a typical pond of mosquito larvae for 45 days **(1 mark)** • draining stagnant ponds is impossible in tropical climates where it can rain heavily most days **(1 mark)** • anti-malarial drugs can have unpleasant side-effects **(1 mark)** so may prevent people from completing the whole course, increasing the likelihood of the disease developing **(1 mark)** • vaccine trials have shown a 56% drop in malaria in children **(1 mark)** however this can give people a false sense of confidence and they stop using bed nets **(1 mark)** • larvae-eating fish adds extra protein to people's diets. **(1 mark)** Or any other valid point.
3. (a)	Award **1 mark** for an impact of climate change. Award further marks for development of each impact. Award marks for both positive and negative impacts. Award **2 marks** where candidates give specific, appropriate named examples which further develop the answer.	12	Possible answers might include: • sea level rises caused by thermal expansion of the oceans **(1 mark)** and also by the melting of glaciers and land-based ice caps **(1 mark)** • low-lying coastal areas will suffer flooding, **(1 mark)** for example, Bangladesh **(1 mark)** leading to large-scale displacement of people **(1 mark)** and loss of land for farming and destruction of property **(1 mark)** • climate change refugees moving to higher ground or to other countries **(1 mark)** from areas such as Tuvalu or the Maldives **(1 mark)** will exert more pressure on resources such as housing, water and power supplies in the receiving area **(1 mark)** • more extreme and more variable weather such as flooding and droughts, **(1 mark)** and more frequent and intense hurricanes due to increased sea temperatures **(1 mark)** • globally, an increase in precipitation, particularly in the winter in northern countries **(1 mark)** • increase in extent of tropical/vector borne diseases, as warmer areas expand. **(1 mark)** Possibly up to 40 million more people in Africa being exposed to risk of contracting malaria **(1 mark)** • longer growing seasons in many areas in northern Europe, **(1 mark)** increasing food production and range of crops being grown **(1 mark)**

Question			General marking instructions for this type of question	Max mark	Specific marking instructions for this question
			(continued)		• predicted extinction of at least 10% of land species, **(1 mark)** and coral reefs suffer 80% bleaching. **(1 mark)** When water is too warm, corals expel the algae living in their tissues causing the coral to turn completely white **(2 marks)** • changes to ocean current circulation may mean the thermohaline circulation starts to lose impact on north-western Europe, resulting in considerably colder winters **(2 marks)** • a more frequent El Niño/La Niña **(1 mark)** leads to changes in the monsoon **(1 mark)** • a prolonged dry season can lead to forest fires, **(1 mark)** for example California **(1 mark)** • the North-West Passage **(1 mark)** will be opened up to ships due to melting sea ice **(1 mark)** meaning more efficient trading routes. **(1 mark)** Or any other valid point.
	(b)	(i) and (ii)	Award **1 mark** for each description of a strategy. Award **1 mark** for each evaluative point. Award **1 mark** each for further developed/ detailed evaluative comments. Award **a maximum of 5 marks** for descriptive points. Do not award marks for reversals. Award **1 mark** where candidates provide specific named examples which further develop the answer.	8	Points may include: • the Thames Flood Barrier **(1 mark)** is a series of gates which can be raised across the river to prevent sea water flooding London. **(1 mark)** This has successfully protected London from flooding on numerous occasions. **(1 mark)** However, a second barrier may be needed to cope with flooding beyond 2070 **(1 mark)** • advance warning systems need to be further developed to advise householders of the potential risks of flooding **(1 mark)** • the UK has implemented hose-pipe bans to reduce water usage in drought periods **(1 mark)** but these are unpopular and difficult to enforce **(1 mark)** • a desalination plant has been built in London to provide additional fresh water in drought. **(1 mark)** This uses 100% renewable energy to operate **(1 mark)** however some feel the money should have been invested in reducing water wastage **(1 mark)** • Scotland is reducing greenhouse emissions by increasing energy production from renewables **(1 mark)** which were meeting 50% of the demand by the end of 2015. **(1 mark)** Or any other valid point.
4.	(a)	(i) and (ii)	Award **1 mark** for each description of a trend. Award **1 mark** for each reason. Award up to **3 marks** for description points.	10	Points may include: • the biggest increase in energy demand is taking place in China **(1 mark)** which requires lots of energy to construct infrastructure **(1 mark)** • an increase in population growth in South-East Asia and China **(1 mark)** leads to increased demands for electricity for lighting and appliances such as televisions. **(1 mark)** Industry in China is based on energy-hungry manufacturing industries **(1 mark)**

Question			General marking instructions for this type of question	Max mark	Specific marking instructions for this question
			(continued)		• in a global economy many of the manufactured products are sold to developed countries, **(1 mark)** and therefore oil is used to transport these around the world **(1 mark)** • Asia's consumption has risen by around 1000 MTOE. **(1 mark)** This may be due to a large increase in passenger air travel **(1 mark)** which has led to the construction of a large number of airport terminals and increased aeroplane use, particularly in South-East Asia **(1 mark)** • as people in developing countries become more prosperous, **(1 mark)** car ownership rates will also increase **(1 mark)** • the smallest increase is in South America/Africa. **(1 mark)** This is due to lower levels of industrialisation **(1 mark)** • energy consumption in developing countries is still increasing, however it is slowing down **(1 mark)** due to attempts to tackle global climate change. **(1 mark)** Or any other valid point.
	(b)		Award **1 mark** for each point on effectiveness. Candidates must discuss a renewable source of energy. Award **0 marks** for non-renewable sources of energy. Award **2 marks** for specific, appropriate named examples which further develop the answer.	10	Possible answers for all renewable energy sources might include: • struggle to meet demand of energy at peak times **(1 mark)** such as early evening due to rise in use of home appliances for evening meals **(1 mark)** • output is variable and depends on the weather conditions. **(1 mark)** This means that there are times when more energy is available than is required which might be difficult to store, **(1 mark)** whilst at other times turbines may be switched off due to over-production **(1 mark)** • electricity may be lost in transferring from areas of production to areas of higher demand/population. **(1 mark)** For hydroelectric power (HEP) other possible answers could include: • even countries like Norway have to import electricity from Sweden during drier months **(1 mark)** • run-of-the-river power stations rely on the flowing water of a river **(1 mark)** and when the river is in spate potential power production is lost **(1 mark)** • conventional HEP stations dam the river to create capacity, however this floods large areas of land **(1 mark)** such as Three Gorges **(1 mark)** which has social consequences such as displacement of people **(1 mark)** • turbines can be easily and cheaply added to water storage reservoirs **(1 mark)** allowing power to be generated from pre-existing infrastructure **(1 mark)** • pump-storage dams effectively allow power to be stored, **(1 mark)** for example Ben Cruachan, **(1 mark)** as water is pumped to an upper reservoir at times of low demand. **(1 mark)** This water can then be released at times of higher demand to generate energy. **(1 mark)** Or any other valid point.

Section 2: Application of Geographical Skills

Question		General marking instructions for this type of question	Max mark	Specific marking instructions for this question
5.	(a) and (b)	Candidates should make reference to all sources, including the Ordnance Survey map, when discussing the suitability of the site and the social, economic and environmental impacts of the housing development on the surrounding area. Award **1 mark** for each description of the site, or explanation of suitability of the site. Award **1 mark** for each impact, and award a further mark where the candidate develops this. Award **1 mark** where candidates refer to the resource and award a further mark where the candidate offers an explanation of its suitability (beyond the wording of the resource). Award up to **4 marks** for map evidence which may include correct and appropriate grid references and/or place/road names. It is possible that some points referred to as a disadvantage may be interpreted by other candidates as a negative impact. Award marks for each point only once, where it is best explained. Candidates may expand on impacts in various ways, for example they may explain impacts of flooding as social, economic *and* environmental.	20	Possible advantages of the location: • the site is located close to a number of transport links **(1 mark)** such as the M5 to the east **(1 mark)** leading to Weston-super-Mare which will allow for commuting **(1 mark)** • the location is less than 1 km from the railway station. **(1 mark)** (322470). **(1 mark)** this may appeal to a wide range of home buyers who may not wish to rely on a car for transport **(1 mark)** • the site is located on a large expanse of flat land **(1 mark)** and this, combined with ease of access, will lower construction costs **(1 mark)** • the site may also appeal to families as it is within driving distance of leisure activities **(1 mark)** such as Exmoor National Park **(1 mark)** • the site is also close to opportunities for scenic walks **(1 mark)** such as the River Parrett Trail **(1 mark)** • there will be an increase in demand for housing **(1 mark)** due to the employment opportunities created by the new power station. **(1 mark)** Possible disadvantages of the location: • the site which has been chosen lies less than 10 metres above sea level, **(1 mark)** therefore this area may be at risk of flooding in heavy rainfall **(1 mark)** • the area chosen is a floodplain **(1 mark)** and this may require expensive flood defences **(1 mark)** • the building of this development may also increase the risk of flooding in surrounding areas **(1 mark)** as run-off will increase from the development due to increase in impermeable surfaces **(1 mark)** • the development lies between a railway line and a main road **(1 mark)** leading to possible air and noise pollution **(1 mark)** • some residents may be concerned about possible safety issues **(1 mark)** relating to transport of radioactive material or waste from the nearby power station. **(1 mark)** Impacts may include: • the increase in houses will help relieve pressure on the local housing markets **(1 mark)** which may have a shortage as a result of people moving into the area due to construction of the power station, **(1 mark)** and because the population in the area has increased by 18,000 between 1991 and 2011 **(1 mark)** • residents of Alstone, GR314468, **(1 mark)** may be unhappy that their quiet rural way of life may be disturbed by a large new housing development on their doorstep **(1 mark)** • construction companies will be attracted to this area **(1 mark)** creating a number of skilled jobs boosting the local economy. **(1 mark)** The increased risk of flooding may mean a rise in insurance premiums. **(1 mark)** Increased population may lead to improved income for local small businesses **(1 mark)** • the building of this development may bring an increase in traffic and congestion on roads **(1 mark)** as the increase in car owners may lead to more noise and air pollution **(1 mark)** • new flood defences may have an adverse consequence on nesting birds/aquatic wildlife in the surrounding area. **(1 mark)** Or any other valid point.

Acknowledgements

Permission has been sought from all relevant copyright holders and Hodder Gibson is grateful for the use of the following:

An extract from "Lake District Management Plan — State of the Park Report 2005: Access and Recreation" © Lake District National Park Authority (2016 page 4);

The table 'Trade Patterns of Selected Countries' taken from the CIA World Fact Book 2013 (https://www.cia.gov/library/publications/the-world-factbook/index.html). Public domain (2016 page 12);

An extract © Sussex Wildlife Trust (2016 page 14);

Two images © Department of Transport. Contains public sector information licensed under the Open Government Licence v3.0 (https://www.nationalarchives.gov.uk/doc/open-government-licence/version/3/) (2016 page 15);

Image © Authentic travel/Shutterstock.com (2018 page 4);

Image 'Meander in the River Clyde' by Colin Inverarity © Copyright Colin Inverarity and licensed for reuse under creativecommons.org./licenses/by-sa.2.0 (2018 SQP Physical and Human Environments page 2);

Image of a ribbon lake is taken from http://wicklowcountywalks.com/images2/glendalough/3glendalough/hd/DSCN3904.JPG © Cedric McCrossan, Wicklow County Walks (2018 SQP Physical and Human Environments page 4);

Image © gary yin/Shutterstock.com (2018 SQP Physical and Human Environments page 7);

An extract from "World Malaria Report 2015", Country-level trends in malaria incidence and mortality, page 14. Copyright 2015 WHO (2018 SQP Global Issues and Geographical Skills page 2);

An extract © Yeovil Express (Newsquest) (2018 SQP Global Issues and Geographical Skills page 6);

Ordnance Survey maps © Crown Copyright 2018. Ordnance Survey 100047450.